THE REAL
JERK

THE REAL JERK

NEW CARIBBEAN CUISINE

LILY & ED POTTINGER

ARSENAL PULP PRESS

VANCOUVER

THE REAL JERK: New Caribbean Cuisine
Copyright © 2002 by Lily & Ed Pottinger

ARSENAL PULP PRESS
103-1014 Homer Street
Vancouver, B.C.
Canada V6B 2W9
arsenalpulp.com

The publisher gratefully acknowledges the support of the Government of Canada
through the Book Publishing Industry Development Program for its publishing activities.

Book and cover design by Lisa Eng-Lodge
Production assistance by Judy Yeung
Edited by Melva McLean with Brian Lam
Food photography by Greg Athans
Food styling by Nathan Fong
Printed and bound in Canada

NATIONAL LIBRARY OF CANADA CATALOGUING IN PUBLICATION DATA:
Pottinger, Lily
The Real Jerk

ISBN 1-55152-115-6

1. Cookery, Caribbean. 2. Real Jerk (Restaurant) I. Pottinger, Ed. II. Title.
TX716.A1P67   2002   641.5'09713'541   C2002-910832-2

CONTENTS

Introduction 7

Cooking Tips 15

Sauces, Salsas, Dips, and Dressings 19

Soups and Salads 31

Fish 47

Seafood 65

Meat and Poultry 77

Side Dishes 107

Breads and Snacks 127

Desserts 143

Drinks 163

Menu Ideas 175

Glossary 177

Index 184

ACKNOWLEDGEMENTS

There are so many people to thank for showing their support and whom we have come to know and respect and appreciate.

We would like to thank God for his many blessings, all the doors he has open and for the paths he has led us. We would also like to thank our wonderful customers for their support over the past eighteen years; Fred Challenger, who gave us a place to live when we couldn't find one; Greg Lawson, for his moral support; Ann Pottinger, for her encouragement, and for being a supportive family member; to mama Carmen Cole and mom Olive Gouldbourne, for their continuous prayers and open ears; Will and Siva, for their input; and all the great Real Jerk staff.

We would like to give special thanks to Miss P, chef at The Real Jerk, who has never failed to give 100 percent, and Natalie Williams, who drives us crazy but never fails to deliver the goods, for her contributions to this book and for being a loyal employee. We would also like to recognize those whose help in the early days of the Jerk has never been forgotten: Paula Munch and Reenie Keely, for designing the Jerk, and "Easy" Ed, who loaned us $300 for the restaurant the day we met him. Also, in 1996, when we were faced with a do-or-die situation, a couple whom we had known briefly, Mike and Susie Kalintiz, blessed us in an incredible way, and we will always be indebted to them for their kindness.

Ed and I are delighted to give our gratitude to Blaine Kyllo, whose suggestion for this book has finally given me the ability to start and finish a project for the first time. (I am the jack-of-all-trades, but master of none!) Thanks, Blaine. We would also like to say a special thank you to Brian Lam, Mel McLean, and the Arsenal Pulp Press family for their trust, patience, and giving us this opportunity to present *The Real Jerk* to you.

Last but not least, we thank our three wonderful children, Troy, Cleigh, and June, whom God blessed us with, and who provide us with the inspiration to get up and "go go" every day

And for all those who have crossed our paths and provided positive inspiration: *Irie!*

INTRODUCTION

LILY: I was the third child in a family of ten. I was an independent-minded and happy child, and I learned at an early age that I would probably have to work hard if I was going to be successful. By the age of six, I was already helping with washing, cooking, farming, and marketing for the family. With so many children in the house, space was at a premium. Privacy was rare. Still, my mother always told me that I was special; as a treat, she often left a piece of coconut toto or roasted breadfruit, wrapped in a towel, at the bottom of the dining-room cabinet, that was just for me.

I have many happy memories of growing up in Jamaica: going to the river to catch crawfish; waking up early to fetch water for the family's breakfast; picking pimentos during the summer on a large farm run by "Mr. Nick"; cooking on the beach with family and friends.

On Fridays, my father always brought fresh fish home, and my mom either fried it up or she'd make a big, simmering pot of fish soup. Mom made a different meal every day of the week, always using vegetables that were in season, and whatever meat and fish were available. Our family also raised chickens and pigs; what we didn't sell or give away, we used for ourselves.

In addition to learning how to cook at home, I was inspired at school by my Home Economics teacher, Miss Tucken, who taught me how to be a creative cook. Along with home economics, I also specialized in business. This combination would help me a lot when Ed and I decided to open a restaurant.

ED: I was born in Jamaica, but my family moved to England when I was five. Still, I have vivid childhood memories of the Island, especially of waiting on the beach for my grandfather to return from fishing, all the while trying to run away from the snapping sand crabs around me. To this very day, I won't eat crabs because of this!

My parents found England a difficult and quite hostile place to live. As a result, our home life was very important. Meals were special times, although I remember disliking Saturdays because that was soup day, and I didn't like soup. But I could always look forward to the next day, Sunday, which meant a big meal — chicken, rice and peas, and fresh vegetables. One Sunday night, I ate so much and asked for more. My mother looked at me skeptically and asked if I could handle it. When I said "yes," she marched me downstairs and made me eat a whole box of dry, saltine crackers.

After that, I learned to be happy with what was on my plate, to not ask for more! However, it didn't stop me from becoming a chicken thief. Where we lived, we shared the kitchen with two other families; we didn't share meals, just the facilities. The preparation of Sunday dinner usually started the night before — chickens were fried and allowed to marinate in seasonings overnight. I soon learned to sneak into the kitchen during the night and raid the chicken pots, taking a leg here, a leg there. This went on for some time until people started to complain about their one-legged chickens. Eventually, I was found out, and my poor butt paid the price!

In the late 1970s, I returned to Jamaica — a young man eager to help my Uncle Barry with his import/export business. I promptly fell in love with the island all over again. I remember being surprised by the smiles on everyone's faces; they had a joy for life, no matter what they were doing. I learned that the slow, easy pace of life is the best way to live.

I first saw Lily when she was walking home from school in St. Ann's. For me, it was love at first sight, but I was too nervous to approach her, so I watched her walk home every day — for months! On her way home, she would always go down the street and go into a store near the gas station; I was sure she had a boyfriend there, but to my relief I learned her father had a sign-making studio there.

Opposite the gas station was the town's police headquarters. The local cops would hang out in front, watching all the pretty girls go by. One day, one of the cops beckoned Lily to approach, and he whispered something to her. I watched with my heart in my mouth, but was ecstatic when Lily gave him a really nasty look and marched off. After that, I made sure that I got introduced to her. I was afraid someone else would win her heart before I did. I played it cool, because not only did I have to win her over, I had to win over her parents, four brothers, and five sisters.

General Patton had nothing on me. I would show up at opportune times and give her rides to the market or to school. Food played an important role in our courtship. I often bought homemade pudding or toto from the stands at St. Ann's Bay and brought them to Lily. I was brilliant, and Lily became mine. It wasn't long after we met that I opened up Little River Jerk, and Lily and I ran it. It was our first foray into the restaurant business.

LILY: Well, Ed went to Canada in 1980 — his parents were already there — and he found work. I stayed behind in Jamaica, but Ed kept pestering me to follow him. In 1981, I decided to take a trip to Canada. Ed convinced me to stay and to marry him, and we've been together ever since. But I was homesick for Jamaica — being away from my family and in a new environment was very scary. In fact, I didn't unpack my bags for over a year, until I felt I was truly ready to embrace my new life. But Ed encouraged and supported me all the way.

ED: I worked for General Motors, but after a few years I started to feel frustrated. I felt I needed to get away and work at something I really loved. At this time, Lily and I lived in Milton, about forty miles outside of Toronto. We'd just had our first son, Troy, and had purchased our first house. Still, I wasn't happy. This led me to sit down one day and write down a list of all the things Lily and I were good at doing, and all the things we didn't want to do. We kept referring to the wonderful experience we had running Little River Jerk back in Jamaica. I knew Lily was an excellent cook, and that I was good with people and also had some business smarts.

One day I left home and returned with a restaurant to our name. Lily didn't believe me. Also, she'd just gotten a cashier's job at the local supermarket and didn't want to leave it. For two weeks I begged her to help me, reassuring her that it would work out in the end. She finally gave in, and we opened The Real Jerk. We started out with meager supplies — paper plates, plastic forks, Styrofoam cups. Our first day's sales amounted to $20, enough to put gas in the car and go home. Every cent we made went into the restaurant. While those early years were hard, in truth we wouldn't have wanted it any other way because we learned about the business from the inside out, and no one can ever take that away from us.

LILY: In those early days of the restaurant, Ed would actually stand outside on the sidewalk offering free food and drinks to passersby, trying to entice them to try Jamaican cuisine. At that time, it was difficult to sell the concept of "jerk food" to Toronto; the only "jerk" people knew was the Steve Martin movie "The Jerk"! But Ed has always had a great rapport with people. He was able to bring in the customers, many of whom are customers to this very day. As time went by, people became more accustomed to the idea of Jamaican food. At the same time, Jamaica became a prime tourist destination for North Americans, and they returned home familiar with the food and the culture. Today in North America, it isn't hard to find a Jamaican or Caribbean restaurant in large urban centers.

ED: The best part of running any successful restaurant is not being really aware that it's a success — I mean, it's always so challenging that there is never time to pat ourselves on the back for a job well done. Maybe one day we can look back and say, "Wow, we actually did it," but for us the most enjoyable thing is seeing the looks on people's faces as they leave our restaurant. They're happy and satisfied. When I opened the restaurant, I wanted to appeal to people's five senses: the rich smell of the spices; the comforting sounds of reggae; the vibrant sight of the art murals on our walls; and the explosive taste and velvety quality of the food — and by those looks on people's faces, I think we do that.

LILY: We have three children — two boys, now nineteen and seventeen, and a ten-year-old daughter. We have instilled in each of our children first to love God, but also to love and respect each other, to be resourceful, thankful, and respectful, and to always tell the truth, even if it hurts. They have also learned never to take anything for granted.

Our kids enjoy most of the Jamaican dishes we make, such as oxtail, beef patties, ackee and codfish, and many more. Because they were born and raised in Canada, we make sure to expose them to every aspect of our culture. They are not particularly interested in following in our footsteps because they think we work too hard! But my daughter in particular enjoys cooking, and whenever I am in the kitchen she is there by my side, willing to help. She likes to bake cookies, make dumplings, and fry plantains.

Our hope is that whatever career paths they choose, they live and work honestly, and give their best effort, no matter what.

ED AND LILY:

"Irie" is a wonderful Jamaican word that is seen on the back of our Real Jerk t-shirts and on the walls of our restaurant. It is similar to the Hawaiian "aloha" in that it has many meanings, but is used primarily as a salutation, as a term of affection and courtesy. This is how we feel about our food, our customers, and our homeland.

There is a gentle, easy rhythm to life in Jamaica that is evident in its people, its culture, and its food. It is this same rhythm that guides us in our restaurant, and which we hope encourages you in your own kitchen. As Jamaicans, food has always been a big part of our life and our culture. Jamaica's motto, "Out of many, one people," describes the rich diversity of life and people there, and also relates to how food, among other things, brings us closer together.

It is our goal to introduce you all to the wonderful world of Jamaican cuisine, whether you visit our restaurant or try our recipes at home. Our hope for this book is that it inspires people to cook, especially young people, and that it gives a positive view of our Caribbean culture. We all have so much in common and, when and if we allow ourselves to be open-minded and take the time to explore our differences, we are so much better for it.

Irie!

COOKING TIPS

Cooking with Spices and Herbs

Using not only fresh herbs but also dried herbs and powdered spices can enhance the taste of Caribbean cooking. Dried herbs and spices are more concentrated in flavor than fresh herbs. For the most part, 1 tbsp of a fresh herb equals $1/2$ to 1 tsp dried and $1/4$ tsp ground. Herbs and spices should be stored in a cool, dark place.

Jamaican cooking also makes use of prepared canned foods, and bottled essences and sauces. For extra flavor and richness to soups, add soup mixes. To stews, chicken and fish dishes, add instant boullion (in sachet or cube form) directly into the pot. Ketchup, HP Sauce, Pikappeppa Sauce, Worcestershire sauce, and soy sauce are also common to our cooking. To add flavor to drinks: add bitters, strawberry, or cherry syrup.

Preparing Provisions and Staples

In Jamaica, we tend to call food staples, "provisions." Yams, coco, sweet potato, green bananas, and breadfruit are all popular provisions used throughout the islands with a variety of dishes. They are readily available and easily prepared. Just peel, cut, or slice, put in a pot with just enough water to cover, add 1 tsp oil, salt to taste, and boil for 20 minutes. When preparing any provisions or banana using oil to grease the palm or you hands this will prevent staining or itching of hands.

Cutting up a Whole Chicken and/or Deboning Chicken Breasts

With a sharp knife, cut off wings by cutting through the wing joints, following the crook of the joints. To cut off legs, cut skin between leg and body, then make a cut through meat along the line between the tail and hip joint. Pull leg away from bone and cut through. If you want to sever the drumsticks from the thighs, cut along the fat line that crosses the joint between drumstick and thigh. Separate backbone by holding body down and cutting along each side of the backbone through the rib joints. To debone the breast, place breast skin side down and cut through cartilage at the V-joint of the neck. Using two hands, bend both sides of breast back and pull, popping out the bone and attached cartilage.

Handling Hot Peppers

The heat of peppers is concentrated in the seeds and veins. When seeding and chopping hot peppers, wear kitchen or rubber gloves. After handling peppers, wash hands thoroughly in warm, soapy water, or soak them in a sugar/water solution. When using whole peppers in soups and stews, or puréeing them in food processors or blenders, the vapor coming off the peppers can be strong, so watch that you don't get the steam in your eyes.

Preparing Sterilized Jars

Jars must be glass and in good condition, without chips or cracks. They must be sterilized.

To sterilize, fill, and seal jars:

a) In a dishwater, use rinse cycle and the hottest temperature. DO NOT use detergent.

b) Place clean jars face down in a large pot, cover completely with cold water. Bring water a to boil, cover pot, and boil jars for 20 minutes. Wearing rubber gloves, and using tongs, remove jars from water.

c) Fill jars with hot liquid. Seal with lacquer-lined sealing seals sold specifically for home preserving. Do not use metal seals, especially when preserving hot peppers — the lids may corrode over time! Place lids securely over seals. Wipe jars clean; turn upside down for a few hours, then test lid and seal. Place in a cool, dark place. Once opened, the jars of preserves must be stored, covered, in a refrigerator.

Buying Fresh Fish

Look for bright, clear eyes on fresh fish as well as flesh, which springs back when you press it. The smell should be fresh (i.e.,no smell). Place fresh fish in the coldest part of the fridge. Freeze any fish you do not intend to use within two days.

Buying and Preparing Shrimp

When buying shrimp, look for a fresh smell like an ocean breeze. Fresh shrimp should not smell "fishy."

Shrimp comes in many sizes. Small (sometimes called salad shrimp), medium, large, and jumbo are the most common sizes of shrimp. The size is determined by how many shrimp, shells on, are found in a pound. Average amounts:

Small: over 40 shrimp per lb
Medium: 35 to 40 shrimp per lb
Large: 26 to 35 shrimp per lb
Jumbo: 20 to 25 shrimp per lb

Peeling and Deveining Shrimp

Using your hands, peel shells starting at the underside, along the feelers. If the intestinal vein that runs along the back is visible (black), remove it with the tip of a sharp paring knife.

Butterflying Shrimp

Cut shrimp down the back to the tip of the tail, keeping shell and shrimp intact. Lift shrimp slightly above shell so that it looks like a large butterfly.

Preparing Mussels

Scrub mussels to remove exterior sand and dirt. Steam in water, broth, or stew until they open; discard any unopened mussels.

Preparing Salt Cod

Cover with cold water and soak overnight. Drain and simmer for 15 minutes. Drain again then simmer one more time. Drain, then remove skin and bones. Flake with a fork. Prepare extra cod, remove bones, and package in freezer bags for ready use in various dishes.

Buying and Preparing Coconut

Choose a heavy coconut. Hold it to your ear and shake. If you hear water sloshing inside, it's a good one! Poke out the eyes with a clean screwdriver or ice pick. Drain the coconut water inside. With a hammer, smash coconut into half a dozen pieces. With a paring knife, pry meat away from the shell and trim brown, hairy skin from the meat.

Buying and Pitting Mangoes

Mangoes are ripe when you press your thumb against the skin and it yields to your pressure. They can be purchased green and ripened at room temperature. With a sharp paring knife, peel mango and pare it as you would a peach, slicing against the pit.

Deep-frying

You can deep-fat fry in a deep fryer, a wok, or even a high-sided skillet. A large, heavy, saucepan, which usually comes high-sided, is ideal because you can rest a thermometer against the side. The average temperature to be reached in deep-frying is 360°F. .

Sauces Salsas Dips & Dressings

THE REAL JERK SAUCE

The technique of jerking is thought to originate with the "Maroons," West African slaves who escaped their Spanish masters to live in remote mountain areas of Jamaica. Later they fought the British, who arrived to re-colonize Jamaica after the Spanish left to search for gold in Central and South America. Because they were always on the run, the Maroons devised a way of spicing and slow cooking pork. The meat was marinated in an exotic mixture of Scotch bonnet peppers, pimento (allspice) berries, escallion, thyme, and other secret ingredients.

After marinating, the meat was cooked over an outdoor pit, about a foot deep. Charcoal from old, burned pimento trees was shoveled into the pit and then the pit was lined with fresh pimento wood. The low, sustained heat from the coals allowed the meat to cook slowly so that it lost little of its natural juices.

In the last two decades, "jerking" has taken the world by storm. There are scores of different jerk sauces and seasonings available in your local supermarkets, but there's nothing like homemade jerk sauce. The secret to the success of The Real Jerk restaurant, and all our jerk recipes, starts with our own jerk sauce. We are pleased to reveal our "secret" recipe with our customers and readers.

1 lb Scotch bonnet peppers

1 small onion, chopped

3 stalks escallion, chopped

3 sprigs fresh thyme, chopped

3 tbsp salt

2 tbsp black pepper

2 tbsp whole pimento (allspice) berries

1 tbsp ground ginger

1 tsp nutmeg, freshly grated

½ cup white vinegar

¼ cup soy sauce

In a food processor or blender, purée all ingredients until the sauce is coarse, yet pourable.

Makes about 4 to 5 cups.

Scotch bonnet peppers are fiery little devils. Wear rubber gloves when seeding or chopping them. After handling, try not to touch your eyes or mouth, and wash your hands thoroughly. Also be careful not to inhale the fumes when you lift the lid off a food processor or blender.

COCONUT MILK

You will notice that many of our recipes use coconut milk. Coconut milk is not the liquid found in coconuts. That's coconut water. Coconut milk, along with other food staples, was introduced into Jamaica by indentured slaves from India who were brought to the Caribbean to work the plantations after the abolition of slavery.

Coconut milk is made by combining coconut meat and hot water to create a liquid that acts like a dairy product. Before the days of refrigeration, coconut milk (often stored in empty coconut shells) was the only dairy-like substance that was safe to use. Coconut milk still takes the place of dairy products in many Caribbean dishes and beverages.

2 cups coconut meat, chopped
1¼ cups warm water

To prepare the coconut, poke out the eyes with a clean screwdriver
 or ice pick.
Drain the coconut water inside.
Using a hammer, smash the coconut into half a dozen pieces.
With a paring knife, pry meat away from the shell and trim brown,
 hairy skin from the meat.
In a food processor or blender, purée the coconut with the water.
Strain the mixture through a sieve or cheesecloth, squeezing all the
 liquid from the mixture.

Makes 1½ cups.

Fresh coconut milk should be your first choice when cooking, but you can any use ready-made forms: canned, liquid, frozen, powdered, or in a solid block form.

When buying a fresh coconut, look for a heavy one. Hold it to your ear and shake it. If you can hear the water sloshing inside, it's a good one.

RUNDOWN SAUCE

When you see "Rundown Mackerel" or "Rundown Shrimp" on the menu of a Caribbean restaurant, it refers to the coconut sauce, called "rundown," that has traditionally been a primary base for many Caribbean dishes, especially for times when meat was scarce. We use rundown sauce in many of our recipes.

2 cups coconut milk (p. 21)
1 tbsp salt
1 cup water
1 large onion, sliced
1 stalk escallion, chopped
2 medium tomatoes, chopped
6 whole pimento (allspice) berries
1 whole Scotch bonnet pepper

In a medium saucepan over high heat, combine coconut milk, salt, and water and boil for 15 minutes until sauce begins to thicken.
Lower heat and stir in remaining ingredients.
Let simmer for 10 minutes.
Remove allspice berries and Scotch bonnet pepper before using.

Makes about 1¹/₂ cups.

SEAFOOD SAUCE

This is one of our favorite sauces to serve with Codfish Fritters (p. 50).

1 cup ketchup
1 tbsp mayonnaise
1 tbsp onion, finely chopped
¼ tsp fresh thyme, chopped

1 tbsp lime juice
1 tbsp Worcestershire sauce
½ tsp hot pepper sauce
½ tsp fresh garlic, grated

In a bowl, whisk all ingredients together.
Cover and refrigerate for at least 4 hours before serving.

Makes about 1¹/₄ cups.

BASIC WHITE SAUCE

We use this classic sauce with many of our fish dishes.

1½ cup milk
3 tbsp cornstarch
½ tsp salt
3 tbsp butter

In a bowl, whisk milk and cornstarch until smooth.
In a saucepan over low heat, cook mixture until it thickens, stirring constantly.
Add salt and butter and cook sauce another 8 to 10 minutes.

Makes about 1¼ cups.

Serving Variations:

Prepare sauce as indicated and during the last 5 minutes:
Add 1 small onion, a sprig of fresh thyme, and one stalk escallion,
    all chopped.
Add 1 small onion, chopped, 1 tsp dried thyme and ½ tsp ground allspice.
Add ½ cup mushrooms and 1 small onion, both chopped,
    along with 1 tsp white pepper.
Add ¼ cup tomatoes, 2 tbsp tomato sauce, 1 tsp black pepper,
    1 tsp dried thyme.

JERK RIB SAUCE

A wonderful, piquant sauce for those juicy ribs!

2 19-oz cans tomato sauce
½ cup water
½ cup brown sugar
1 tsp black pepper
1 tsp ground allspice
1 tsp fresh ginger, grated or ½ tsp ground ginger
2 cloves fresh garlic, finely chopped
1 small onion, cut in half
1 tbsp fresh thyme, chopped
1 tbsp Worcestershire sauce
2 tbsp soy sauce
2 tbsp white vinegar
3 tbsp jerk sauce, or more if you like it hotter (p. 20)
2 tbsp plum sauce (optional)

In a medium saucepan, combine all ingredients except
    jerk sauce and bring to a boil.
Lower heat and let simmer for 15 minutes, stirring frequently.
Remove pan from heat and let cool for 20 minutes.
Remove chunks of spices and stir in jerk sauce.

Makes about 2 cups.

This sauce can be preserved and stored in the refrigerator for up to
3 months. See preserving instructions on (p. 16).

A quick and easy variation is to take 1 bottle of your favorite barbecue
sauce and stir in 3 tbsp jerk sauce, ¹/₂ tsp ground ginger, and ¹/₂ tsp
ground allspice.

ZIPPY DIPPING SAUCE

This sauce is great with Fried Dumplings (p. 139).

1 cup ketchup
1 tsp white vinegar
1 sprig fresh thyme, chopped
2 tbsp sugar
1 tbsp hot pepper sauce
¼ tsp ground ginger
¼ cup water

In a small saucepan over low heat, combine all ingredients and let simmer for 10 minutes.

Cool sauce to room temperature before serving.

Makes about 1¼ cups.

LEMON & LIME SAUCE

Golden Fried Chicken (p. 104) and this sauce? Great!

½ cup sugar   **1 cup water**
1 tbsp cornstarch   **2 tbsp lemon juice**
1 tbsp lime zest   **1 tbsp lime juice**
pinch of salt   **2 tbsp butter**

In a medium saucepan over low heat, combine sugar, cornstarch, lime zest, and salt.

Slowly stir in water, then lemon and lime juice.

Cook for 8 minutes, stirring constantly until sauce thickens.

Remove pan from heat.

Stir in butter until melted.

Cool sauce to room temperature before serving.

Makes about 1 cup.

QUICK VEGETABLE DIP

Whether you're running a busy restaurant or running off to a potluck party, fresh vegetables, chips, or crackers, combined with a tasty dip or salsa make winning appetizers. This simple recipe and the five that follow are some of the favorites at The Real Jerk.

1 cup sour cream
½ cup bottled Ranch dressing
1 sachet (or cube, crumbled) chicken bouillon
black pepper to taste

In a bowl, combine sour cream, dressing, bouillon, and black pepper. Cover and refrigerate at least 2 hours before serving with fresh raw vegetables of your choice.

Makes about 1½ cups.

AVOCADO DIP

This guacamole-like dip can be served with chips and crackers or as a dressing for sandwiches made with Jerk Chicken (p. 99).

2 medium avocados
1 stalk escallion, chopped
1 tsp white vinegar
1 tbsp lime juice
¼ tsp salt
2 tbsp white sugar
black pepper to taste
bacon bits (garnish) (optional)

Halve avocados.
Remove pits and scoop out flesh.
In a bowl, and using a fork, mash flesh.
Mix in remaining ingredients.
Garnish with bacon bits before serving.

Makes about 1¼ cups.

CRAB DIP

1 6-oz can crab meat
½ cup mayonnaise
3 oz cream cheese
¼ cup sour cream
¼ tsp celery salt
1 clove garlic
1 tbsp lime or lemon juice
½ tsp green pepper, finely chopped
¼ tsp onion, grated

In a food processor or blender, purée all ingredients.
Transfer to a bowl, then cover and refrigerate at least 2 hours before serving.

Makes about 1¼ cups.

Serving Variations:

Cut one cucumber lengthwise.
Cut out seeds and flesh to form a boat.
Fill with crab dip just before serving.
Cut cucumber into 1" serving pieces.

CUCUMBER DIP

1 medium cucumber, peeled and finely chopped
1 8-oz pkg soft cream cheese
1 cup sour cream
1 tsp white vinegar
2 tbsp escallion, finely chopped
1 tbsp celery salt
¼ tsp black pepper

In a bowl, combine all ingredients.
Cover and refrigerate for at least 2 hours before serving.

Makes about 1½ cups.

MANGO TANGO SALSA

Both Mango Tango Salsa and the next recipe, Mango and Papaya Salsa, make great condiments for Coconut Shrimp (p. 69) and Jerk Chicken (p. 99).

½ cup ripe mango, diced

2 tbsp onion, diced

½ tsp escallion, diced

2 tbsp green pepper, diced

3 tbsp tomatoes, diced

2 tbsp tamarind dressing (p. 30)

dash of jerk sauce (p. 20)

pinch fresh thyme, chopped (optional)

In a bowl, combine all ingredients.
Cover and refrigerate for at least 2 hours before serving.

Makes about 1¼ cups.

 Mangoes are tropical fruits with red to yellow skins. You can buy them green and ripen at room temperature. Pare mangos just before using and cut against the pit as you would peaches.

MANGO & PAYAYA SALSA

This refreshing salsa keeps in the refrigerator for up to 4 days.

1 cup ripe mango, coarsely chopped

1 cup papaya, coarsely chopped

1 tsp red onion, chopped

2 tbsp green pepper, chopped

4 tbsp sugar

1 tbsp lime juice

3 tbsp red wine vinegar

In a bowl, combine all ingredients.
Cover and refrigerate for at least 2 hours before serving.

Makes about 1½ cups.

COOL GREEN SALAD DRESSING

Serve this one over Tangy Coleslaw (p. 44), Spicy Mixed Bean Salad (p. 45), or your favorite green salad.

½ cup brown sugar

⅓ cup corn oil or olive oil

⅔ cup white vinegar

1 tsp salt or celery salt

¼ tsp black pepper

In a food processor or blender, purée all ingredients.
Transfer to a bowl, cover, and refrigerate at least 2 hours before serving.

Makes about 1 cup.

COOL & CREAMY SALAD DRESSING

This is another quick and easy dressing for any garden salad.

1 cup mayonnaise

4 tbsp ketchup

3 tbsp sugar

2 tbsp white vinegar

In a food processor or blender, purée all ingredients.
Transfer to a bowl, cover, and refrigerate at least 2 hours before serving.

Makes about 1 cup.

TAMARIND DRESSING

Tamarind dressing can be used on salads or as a seafood dip. Tamarind pulp or paste can be found in any Asian or West Indian market, as well as in many large supermarkets.

8 oz tamarind pulp or paste
1 cup hot water
1 clove garlic, chopped
1 small onion, chopped
1 tsp fresh thyme, chopped
1 stalk escallion, chopped

1 tsp salt
½ tsp black pepper
½ cup vegetable oil
¼ cup white vinegar
1 cup red wine vinegar
¼ cup brown sugar

In a bowl, dissolve tamarind pulp in hot water.

Using a sieve, strain and discard pits and larger pieces of pulp.

In a large mixing bowl, combine tamarind juice with the onion, garlic, escallion, thyme, salt and pepper.

Add vegetable oil and mix well.

Blend in remaining ingredients.

Cover and refrigerate for at least 2 hours before serving.

Makes about 3 cups.

This dressing can be kept in the refrigerator for up to 3 days. It can also be preserved. See preserving instructions on p. 16.

AVOCADO DRESSING

½ ripe avocado
1 tsp lemon juice
½ cup sour cream
⅓ vegetable oil
1 clove garlic, minced

½ tsp sugar
½ tsp chili powder
¼ tsp salt
¼ tsp jerk sauce (p. 20)
4 slices cooked bacon, crumbled (optional)

Halve an avocado. Remove pit, peel, and scoop out flesh.

In a food processor or blender, purée avocado flesh with remaining ingredients until smooth.

Transfer to a bowl, cover, and refrigerate at least 2 hours before serving.

Makes about 1¼ cups.

Soups&Salads

CHICKEN STOCK

A good chicken stock is the basis for many soups and stews. You can make this stock in larger amounts and freeze in 1-quart batches.

3 lbs chicken pieces: necks, backs, or wing tips
14 cups water
½ lb onions, each one quartered
½ lb carrot, chopped
2 sprigs fresh thyme
½ tsp whole black peppercorns
1 tsp celery salt
½ tsp whole allspice berries

Wash chicken pieces.
In a large stockpot, bring water to boil.
Add chicken pieces and boil for 15 minutes.
Remove pot from heat, strain, and reserve stock.
Discard bones.
Return stock to pot.
Add vegetables and spices.
Bring back to a boil.
Cover, lower heat, and let simmer for 20 to 30 minutes or
    until chicken is tender and done.
Strain, reserving stock for future use.

Makes about 2 liters.

We always wash our chicken and meat with a liquid make with 1 tsp each of lime juice, white vinegar, and water.

CHICKEN SOUP AT THE JERK

You can substitute celery, turnips, celery root, or rutabaga for the vegetables in this soup.

1 lb chicken pieces: legs, wings, or backs

9 cups water

1 small onion, chopped

2 stalks escallion, chopped

½ lb pumpkin or acorn squash, seeded and chopped

2 medium potatoes, seeded and cubed

1 medium carrot, peeled and chopped

½ lb Jamaican yellow yam, seeded and chopped

½ small cho cho, diced

12 spinners (p. 140)

1 whole Scotch bonnet pepper

2 sprigs fresh thyme

¼ tsp salt

¼ tsp black pepper

1 2-oz pkg chicken noodle soup mix

Wash chicken pieces.

In a large stockpot, bring water to boil.

Add chicken pieces, onion, escallion, and pumpkin and boil for 15 minutes.

Lower heat and let simmer until chicken is tender.

Add remaining ingredients.

Cover and let simmer for another 15 minutes, until vegetables are cooked.

Remove Scotch bonnet pepper and thyme before serving.

Serves 6.

 There are many varieties of yams. Some are hard; some are soft, and both can vary in texture and color. The yellow yam is available in most grocery stores and can be peeled, sliced, boiled, or added to any soup or stew. It is also used in baking.

RED PEA SOUP

Red pea soup is a favorite Jamaican dish, and the flavor differs from kitchen to kitchen, from town to town. This soup is also one of the many soups you can buy in roadside shops. I frequent Pinkey's shop in Port Antonio where having soup is a "hair-raising" experience: it's so good that the hair on the back of your neck stands up in delight. –L.

3 cups raw red kidney beans, washed and soaked overnight
12 cups water
1 lb stewing beef
10 cups water
½ lb yam, peeled and cubed
1 medium potato, peeled and cubed
1 medium carrot, peeled and chopped
1 medium sweet potato, peeled and cubed
10 to 12 spinners (p. 140)
1 cup coconut milk
3 stalks escallion, chopped
4 slices canned breadfruit
1 sprig fresh thyme, chopped
1 whole Scotch bonnet pepper
1 12-oz pkg of chicken or beef soup mix

In a large stockpot, boil stewing beef and red beans until meat is tender.
Add yams, potato, carrot, sweet potato, and spinners and boil for
　　　another 15 minutes.
Stir in remaining ingredients, lower heat, and let simmer for 5 minutes,
　　　stirring occasionally, until vegetables are cooked.
Remove thyme and Scotch bonnet pepper before serving.

Serves 4 to 6.

Because breadfruit is seasonal, canned is often used instead of fresh. For roasting, however, only fresh breadfruit will do.

In Jamaica, we call red kidney beans "red peas." Using raw beans soaked and prepared is the traditional method; you can also use canned kidney beans.

VEGETABLE & RED PEA SOUP

At home, you can add leftover vegetables and turkey bones to this soup for added flavor.

10 cups water
2 19-oz cans red kidney beans
½ cup coconut milk (p. 21)
1 tbsp salt
½ tsp black pepper
10 whole pimento (allspice) berries
1 small onion, chopped
1 large carrot, sliced
2 medium white potatoes, cubed
½ lb Jamaican yellow yam, peeled and cubed
12 spinners (p. 140)
1 2-oz pkg vegetable soup mix
2 stalks escallion, chopped
2 sprigs fresh thyme
¼ small green pepper, seeded and sliced
1 whole Scotch bonnet pepper

In a large stockpot, bring water to a boil.

Add first 7 ingredients and boil for 10 minutes.

Add carrot, potatoes, yam, and spinners and boil another 15 minutes.

Stir in remaining ingredients, lower heat, and let simmer for 15 to 20 minutes, stirring occasionally, until vegetables are cooked.

Remove Scotch bonnet pepper and thyme before serving.

Serves 6 to 8.

PEPPER POT SOUP

Callaloo, a leafy vegetable similar to spinach, is used in pepper pot soup,
a traditional Jamaican dish. Crayfish (or shrimp) added at the end of the cooking
time provides extra flavor.

10 cups water
1½ lb fresh callaloo or spinach (or 2 14-oz cans)
1 medium onion, chopped
2 cloves garlic, chopped
½ cup coconut milk (p. 21)
6 okra, chopped
½ lb yellow yam, peeled and cubed
¼ lb coco, peeled and cubed
1 medium potato, peeled and cubed
1 medium carrot, peeled and chopped
12 spinners (p. 140)
1 2-oz pkg vegetable soup mix
2 sprigs fresh thyme, chopped
2 stalks escallion, chopped
1 whole Scotch bonnet pepper
salt and black pepper to taste

In a large stockpot, combine water, callaloo, onion, garlic, and coconut milk.
Bring to a boil, then lower heat, cover pot, and let simmer for 15 minutes.
Bring heat back up to medium, add okra, yam, coco, potato, and carrot and
 cook for 15 minutes until vegetables are done.
Stir in spinners, soup mix, thyme, escallion, Scotch bonnet pepper, salt, and
 pepper, and let cook for another 15 to 20 minutes.
Remove Scotch bonnet pepper before serving.

Serves 6.

CREAM OF CALLALOO SOUP

You can substitute other leafy vegetables, like spinach or Swiss chard, but if you have a West Indian market near you, try the callaloo. It really does have a lovely, unique flavor.

4 cups water
½ lb fresh callaloo, chopped
1 small onion, chopped
2 tbsp butter
2 tbsp flour
1 cup milk
salt and black pepper to taste
¼ tsp ground allspice
½ tsp jerk sauce (p. 20)

In a stockpot, combine water and callaloo and boil for 10 minutes.

Remove pot from stove and cool mixture slightly.

In a food processor or blender, purée callaloo until smooth and set aside.

In a small bowl, whisk flour and milk together and set aside.

In a saucepan over medium heat, sauté onions in butter for 2 minutes, until opaque.

Add flour and milk mixture, stirring constantly, until sauce thickens.

Add puréed callaloo, salt, pepper, allspice, and jerk sauce and let simmer for 8 to 10 minutes.

Serves 4.

FISH TEA

Yes, this is a soup, although some Jamaicans like to drink it as a tea in a teacup – no spoons! My father drank a cup of Fish Tea at breakfast every Saturday morning. Fish Tea can also be served as an appetizer. –L.

5 cups water
1 lb fish heads
2 small carrots, peeled and chopped
½ small cho cho, peeled and chopped
1 stalk green onion, chopped
1 sprig fresh thyme, chopped
1 whole Scotch bonnet pepper
1 2-oz pkg fish tea soup mix
1 tsp butter
¼ tsp black pepper

In a stockpot, combine water and fish heads and boil for 20 minutes.
Using a sieve, strain stock, removing fish bones.
Add remaining ingredients to stock and cook for another 10 minutes.
Remove Scotch bonnet pepper before serving.

Serves 4.

 Fish tea soup mix can be found in West Indian and Asian markets, but you can also substitute vegetable soup mix.

LOBSTER & SHRIMP BISQUE

A seafood lover's delight, not just in Jamaica, but all around the world.

6 cups water

1 tsp salt

2 6-oz cooked lobster tails, shells on

6 Black tiger shrimp, heads and shells on

2 tbsp vegetable oil

½ cup evaporated milk

1 sprig fresh thyme

1 stalk escallion

1 tsp salt

¼ tsp black pepper

2 tbsp flour

2 tbsp butter

In a large stockpot, bring water and salt to boil.

Add lobster tails.

Cover, lower heat, and let simmer for 8 minutes.

Remove lobster, cut away shells, and reserve for stock.

Cut lobster meat into 1" pieces and set aside.

In a large saucepan over medium heat, fry shrimp in oil for 4 minutes.

Remove shrimp, peel shells, and set aside.

In a stockpot, boil lobster and shrimp shells for 30 minutes.

Strain, discarding shells.

Add remaining ingredients to stock and let simmer over low heat
    for 5 minutes.

In a small bowl, mix milk and flour together to form a smooth paste.

Add paste to stockpot. Let simmer stock another 5 minutes.

Remove sprig of thyme and escallion before serving.

Serves 4.

MANNISH WATER

In the old days, goat was such a special treat that it was reserved for men only (it being a man's world and all). Women were not allowed to eat or cook it. This soup, made from goat, is called Mannish Water not only because only men could drink it, but also because it was widely believed to increase a man's virility.

16 cups water
3 lbs goat head, tripe, and feet
1 tbsp salt
1 lb yellow yam, peeled and cubed
1 medium cho cho, peeled and diced
½ lb coco, peeled and cubed
1 medium potato, peeled and cubed
1 medium carrot, peeled and cubed
4 fingers green banana, peeled and cut in pieces
14 spinners (p. 140)
2 whole Scotch bonnet peppers
2 stalks escallion, chopped
2 sprigs fresh thyme, chopped
1 tsp whole black peppercorns
6 whole pimento (allspice) berries
1 12-oz pkg vegetable soup mix

Rinse meat in water and lime juice.
In a large stockpot, combine water, meat, and salt.
Cook over medium heat for 1 to 1½ hours, until goat meat is tender.
Strain, removing as many bones as possible.
Return stock to pot, add all the vegetables and the banana and
    cook for 20 minutes.
Stir in spinners, Scotch bonnet peppers, escallion, thyme, peppercorns,
    allspice berries, and soup mix.
Cover and let simmer for 15 to 20 minutes, adding extra water if needed.
Remove Scotch bonnet pepper, peppercorns, and allspice berries before serving.

Serves 6 to 8.

You can find goat meat in West Indian, Italian, Portuguese, and Greek markets. When asked, most butchers will be happy to cut up the meat for you.

CRUNCHY SHRIMP SALAD

The celery gives this salad a crunchy texture.

½ lb medium cooked salad shrimp
½ cup mayonnaise
⅓ cup onion, finely chopped
⅓ cup celery, finely chopped
1 tbsp chives, finely chopped
1 pinch fresh thyme
¼ tsp salt
¼ black pepper
¼ tsp hot pepper sauce (optional)
lettuce leaves
1 tomato, thinly sliced

Rinse shrimp and set aside.

In a bowl, whisk mayonnaise until smooth.

Add remaining ingredients, mixing well.

Cover and refrigerate until ready to serve.

To serve, arrange lettuce leaves and tomatoes on top of crackers or bread.

Top with shrimp salad.

Serves 4.

SPICY FISH SALAD

1 8-oz snapper fillet
½ tsp jerk sauce (p. 20)
1 tbsp vegetable oil
4 cups cooked potatoes, diced
2 hard-boiled eggs, finely chopped
½ tsp onions, diced
½ tsp escallion, finely chopped
1 tbsp butter
6 tbsp mayonnaise
½ tsp salt
½ tsp black pepper
sprinkle of paprika (garnish)

Preheat oven to 400°F.

Season fish with oil and jerk sauce.

Bake in a greased casserole for 15 minutes.

Remove from oven, let cool and flake fish with fork.

In a large salad bowl, combine remaining ingredients.

Add fish flakes and serve warm or cold, and sprinkle with paprika, if desired.

Serves 4 to 6.

CUCUMBER SALAD

⅓ cup white vinegar
¼ cup sugar
1 clove garlic, minced
⅓ cup olive oil
salt and black pepper to taste
2 cucumbers, coarsely chopped
1 medium tomato, coarsely chopped

In a large bowl, whisk together vinegar, sugar, garlic, oil, salt, and pepper.

Add cucumbers and tomato and toss.

Cover and refrigerate for at least one hour before serving.

Serves 4 to 6.

CRAB & AVOCADO SALAD

You can't go wrong with a crab salad. You can substitute tomatoes for the avocados in this recipe.

3 ripe avocados
½ cup mayonnaise
½ cup sour cream
¼ cup celery, finely chopped
¼ cup escallion, finely chopped
¼ cup fresh cilantro, finely chopped
¼ cup cayenne pepper
salt and pepper to taste
1 lb cooked crab meat
¼ tsp jerk sauce (p. 20)
cilantro (garnish)

Peel, halve, and remove pits from avocados.

In a medium bowl, combine first seven ingredients.

Fold in crab meat and jerk sauce, mixing as little as
    possible so as not to break up the meat.

Fill avocado halves with mixture.

Garnish with cilantro.

Serves 6.

TANGY COLESLAW

2 cups cabbage, finely shredded

1 medium carrot, coarsely grated

1 tsp white vinegar

4 tbsp Italian salad dressing

1 tsp white sugar

¼ tsp salt

¼ tsp black pepper

In a large bowl, combine cabbage and carrots.

In a separate bowl, whisk together vinegar, dressing, sugar, salt, and pepper.

Add to vegetables. Mix well. Cover and refrigerate until ready to serve.

Serves 4.

CREAMY COLESLAW

4 cups cabbage, finely shredded

½ cup carrots, shredded

½ cup mayonnaise

2 tbsp white sugar

1 tbsp white vinegar

raisins (garnish)

chopped nuts (garnish)

sunflower seeds (garnish)

In a large bowl, combine cabbage and carrots.

In a separate bowl, whisk together mayonnaise, sugar, and vinegar.

Add to vegetables. Mix well. Cover and refrigerate until ready to serve.

Garnish with raisins, nuts, or sunflower seeds, if desired.

Serves 6.

COOL & CREAMY CARROT SALAD

4 cups carrots, coarsely grated
½ cup raisins
¼ cup mayonnaise
¼ tsp white vinegar
1 tbsp white sugar
lettuce leaves

In large bowl, mix all ingredients.
Cover and refrigerate until ready to use.
Serve on a bed of lettuce leaves.

Serves 4.

SPICY MIXED BEAN SALAD

Mixed bean salads always go over well at picnics and potlucks. This recipe is our "Jamaican spin" on a traditional recipe.

1 19-oz can chickpeas, drained
1 19-oz can red kidney beans, drained
1 19-oz can mixed beans, drained
2 stalks celery, sliced
½ cup green pepper, diced
1 small onion, chopped
1 clove garlic, minced
1 green onion, chopped
¼ tsp jerk sauce (p. 20)
1 cup mayonnaise or 1 cup Italian salad dressing

In a large bowl, combine all ingredients.
Cover and refrigerate until ready to serve.

Serves 6 to 8.

POTATO & PASTA SALAD

4 cooked potatoes, cubed

1 cup cooked elbow macaroni

1 tbsp butter

1 clove garlic, minced

1 small onion, finely chopped

¼ cup celery, finely chopped

1 14-oz can green peas, drained

2 hard-boiled eggs, finely chopped

½ cup mayonnaise

salt and black pepper to taste

½ tsp jerk sauce (p. 20)

In a large bowl, combine cooked potatoes and macaroni.

In a saucepan over medium heat, sauté garlic and onions in butter
    until the onions are opaque.

Pour over potato and macaroni mixture.

Add remaining ingredients and mix well.

Serve warm or cold.

Serves 6.

PAPAYA SALAD

1 medium ripe papaya, peeled and diced

1 cup pineapple chunks

1 small onion, finely chopped

1 stalk green onion, finely chopped

1 cup firm ripe mango, diced

3 tbsp vegetable oil

3 tbsp sugar

1 tbsp lime juice, freshly squeezed

salt and black pepper to taste

sprinkle of red onions, chopped (optional)

In a large bowl, combine all ingredients.

Cover and refrigerate at least 2 hours before serving.

Garnish with red onions, if desired.

Serves 4.

Fish

ACKEE & CODFISH

The fruit of a West African tree, ackee was introduced into Jamaica during the 19th century as a way to feed slaves cheaply and with a fruit they were familiar with. Legend has it that Captain Bligh was carrying young ackee plants, along with breadfruit plants, in the hold of the infamous HMS *Bounty*. During the voyage, Bligh ordered that the plants be given a share of the crew's water supply, which eventually ran out and led to the infamous mutiny during which all the plants were thrown overboard. The irony is that the slaves did not like either the ackee or the breadfruit; it took years for them to become accustomed to both. Bligh, however, did succeed in bringing more plants to Jamaica, in another ship of course. What's more, the Latin name for ackee is named after him: *Blighia sapida*.

Ackee is now the national fruit of Jamaica, and Ackee & Cod Fish is Jamaica's national dish. Serve it with Fried Dumplings (p. 139) or Boiled Bananas (p. 126). You can also add leftover Jerk Pork (p. 78) and turn it into a traditional Jamaican breakfast dish. Note: It is illegal to import fresh ackee into North America because the flesh can be poisonous if the fruit is not ripened properly. But canned ackee is perfectly safe!

1 large onion, chopped

3 tomatoes, sliced

1 stalk escallion, chopped

1 lb prepared salt cod
  (see note on p. 17)

¼ cup vegetable oil

2 strips cooked bacon,
  cut into 1" pieces

2 14-oz cans ackee, drained

½ tsp salt

½ tsp black pepper

1 tsp jerk sauce (p#) (optional)

1 whole Scotch bonnet pepper,
  seeded and sliced (optional)

In a large saucepan over medium heat, sauté onions, tomatoes, escallion, and cod in vegetable oil for 3 minutes.

Add bacon, ackees, salt, pepper, jerk sauce, and Scotch bonnet pepper, and sauté another 5 minutes.

Serves 4 to 6.

Salt cod is readily available in larger supermarkets and in West Indian, Italian, Portuguese, and Asian markets. Cod should be fresh smelling and firm.

Use leftover Ackee & Codfish to make Fried Ackee Sandwiches. After spreading mixture on sandwiches, butter outer sides of bread and fry in a skillet until bread is light brown and crispy.

ACKEE & CODFISH PATTIES

You can you freeze these patties before baking, then thaw and bake just before going to a party or potluck dinner.

1 9" pie pastry (p. 144)
1 cup prepared Ackee and Codfish (p. 48)
1 egg yolk
3 tbsp water

Preheat oven to 350°F.

On a lightly floured surface, using a rolling pin, roll out pastry dough
    to form a thin crust.

With a 3" pastry or cookie cutter, cut dough into circles.

Fill each circle with 1 tbsp ackee and cod.

Fold each circle over to form a patty.

To seal edges of patty, dip finger in water and run along edge of dough.

Using a fork, seal by crimping the edges.

Prick tops of patties 2 or 3 times to let steam escape.

In a small bowl, make an egg wash by mixing the egg yolk with water.

Using a pastry brush, lightly brush tops of patties with wash.

Transfer patties to a greased baking sheet and back for 10 to 15 minutes.

Serves 8 to 10.

CODFISH FRITTERS

These traditional codfish fritters can be served with a variety of sauces, including our own Seafood Sauce (p. 22).

1 lb flour
2 tbsp baking powder
1 tsp salt
1 tsp black pepper
1 tsp curry powder (optional)
1 small onion, finely chopped
1 stalk escallion, finely chopped
1 small tomato, coarsely chopped

1 large egg
1½ cups water
**½ lb prepared salt cod
  (see note on p. 17)**
**1 Scotch bonnet pepper, seeded and
  finely chopped (see note on p. 15)**
1 cup vegetable oil

In a large bowl, combine flour, baking powder, salt, pepper,
     and curry powder. Set aside.
In a separate bowl, combine onions, escallion, tomato, egg, and water.
Stir in flour mixture, then add cod, and pepper sauce. Mix well.
In a deep-fryer or large, heavy saucepan, heat oil to 360°F.
Spoon tablespoons of fritter batter, about 5 at a time, into hot oil.
Fry until both sides are light brown and crispy.
Drain on paper towels to absorb excess oil.
Serve hot with your favorite sauce.

Serves 4 to 6.

Back in the days of prohibition, Jamaica and Newfoundland engaged in some profitable, though illegal, trade. Jamaica shipped loads of its empty rum barrels to Newfoundland. Because they were empty, they were never questioned, but once there they enabled Newfoundlanders to produce their own alcohol properly. In return, Newfoundland shipped Grade A cod to Jamaica.

It was a mutually beneficial arrangement, until Newfoundland started shipping lower-grade cod to Jamaica, apparently hoping it wouldn't notice. However, the inferior product began poisoning a number of Jamaicans. Jamaica, in turn, shipped tainted rum barrels to Newfoundland, which poisoned a number of Newfoundlanders. Despite the potentially dangerous situation, trade resumed shortly thereafter without a word said between them. This relationship explains why Jamaica's national dish requires Newfoundland cod, and why Screech, the traditional drink of Newfoundland, is made using rum barrels from Jamaica.

ESCOVITCHED SALT COD

This dish gets its name from the vinaigrette sauce used to cook the cod in. The same escovitch (vinaigrette) is used in the preparation of many fish dishes.

2 lbs salt cod, prepared and flaked (see note on p. 17)

1 cup vegetable oil

1 large onion, sliced

2 Scotch bonnet peppers, seeded & sliced (see note on p. 15)

½ tsp black pepper

3 tbsp white or cider vinegar

½ tsp ground allspice

3 tbsp water

pinch of salt

lime slices or wedges (garnish)

Cut cod into 1" pieces. Set aside.

In a large, heavy saucepan or deep-fryer, heat vegetable oil to 360°F.

Deep-fry cod pieces until golden. Transfer to a serving dish.

Discard half of the oil. To the remaining oil, add remaining ingredients and sauté for 5 minutes.

Pour sauce over cod and serve with lime slices or wedges for garnish.

Serves 4 to 6.

HAM & CODFISH

A wonderful breakfast dish served with Fried Dumplings (p. 139) and hard-boiled eggs.

1 medium onion, sliced

1 large tomato, chopped

2 tsp vegetable oil

1 lb cooked ham, cut into bite-sized pieces

½ lb prepared salt cod (see note on p. 17)

4 strips bacon, cooked and cut into small pieces

¼ tsp Scotch bonnet pepper, seeded and sliced (see note on p. 15)

½ tsp black pepper

1 tbsp ketchup

In a saucepan over medium heat, sauté onions and tomato in oil for 3 minutes.
Add cooked ham and cod and sauté for 5 minutes.
Stir in remaining ingredients and cook for another 3 minutes.

Serves 4.

BRUSSEL SPROUTS & CODFISH

This can be used as a main or a side dish.

1 lb brussel sprouts,
  trimmed and halved

4 cups water

¼ tsp salt

4 tbsp olive oil

1 medium onion, sliced

½ lb prepared salt cod
  (see note on p. 17)

1 tbsp butter

black pepper to taste

In a medium saucepan, boil brussel sprouts in 4 cups of salted water
      for 3 minutes. Drain and set aside.
In a large saucepan over medium heat, sauté onions and cod in oil
      for 2 minutes.
Add brussel sprouts, butter, pepper, and extra water, if needed,
      and sauté for another 3 minutes.

Serves 4.

COO COO or TURN CORNMEAL

This dish is Grenada's national dish. In Jamaica, we call it Turn Cornmeal.

2 cups water
1 cup coconut milk (p. 21)
½ lb prepared salt cod (see note on p. 17)
1 medium onion, chopped
6 whole okra, chopped
1 medium tomato, chopped
1 stalk escallion, chopped
1 sprig fresh thyme, chopped
1 whole Scotch bonnet pepper
1 tsp salt
1 tsp black pepper
1½ cups cornmeal
3 tbsp margarine

In a saucepan over high heat, bring water to boil.
Add coconut milk, cod, onion, okra, tomato, escallion,
thyme, salt and pepper, and Scotch bonnet pepper.
Boil for 8 to 10 minutes. Lower heat.
Stir in cornmeal, mixing well.
Cover pot and let steam for 20 to 30 minutes, stirring occasionally.
Add margarine, remove Scotch bonnet pepper, and serve.

Serves 4 to 6.

 Remember that the fumes from Scotch bonnet peppers can be strong.
When removing lids from pots, try not to inhale the steam.

BROCCOLI & CODFISH

This is my favorite dish when I'm on a diet. –L.

1 small onion, sliced
½ lb prepared salt cod (see note on p. 17)
3 tbsp vegetable oil
1 bunch broccoli, cut into bite-sized pieces and blanched
salt and black pepper to taste

In a large saucepan over medium heat, sauté onions and
   cod in oil for 4 minutes.
Add broccoli, stirring so that it is well blended.
Season with salt and pepper and cook for another 3 minutes.

Serves 2.

STEAMED VEGETABLES & COD

2 small onions, sliced
2 tbsp vegetable oil
1 small cho cho, peeled and sliced
1 large carrot, cut in strips
½ lb prepared salt cod, flaked
1 small green pepper, seeded and cut in strips
¼ cup water
2 tbsp butter
salt and black pepper to taste
½ small cabbage, shredded
1 bunch baby bok choy, chopped

In a large saucepan over medium heat, sauté onions in oil for 2 minutes.
Add carrots and cho cho and cook for another 2 minutes.
Stir in remaining ingredients.
Lower heat, cover, and steam for 10 minutes.

Serves 4.

GRILLED CELERY ROOT & CODFISH

I'd never tried celery root, but after watching it prepared on a TV cooking show, I just had to go get some and create a Caribbean dish with it. I discovered that celery root and cod, grilled on a barbecue, makes a tasty filling for Rotis (p. 131), tortillas, or pita bread. –L.

1½ lb celery root, peeled and sliced into 4 pieces
1 small onion, sliced
3 tbsp olive oil
½ lb prepared salt cod (see note on p. 17)
½ tsp curry powder
pinch ground cumin
2 cloves garlic, chopped
salt and black pepper to taste
¼ cup water

Preheat barbecue or grill to 300°F.
Grill celery root pieces until they begin to soften.
Remove from grill, dice, and set aside.
In a medium saucepan over medium heat, sauté onions and cod and
    in oil for 4 minutes.
Stir in celery root, curry powder, cumin, garlic, salt, pepper, and water.
Cover pot and steam until cooked, about 15 minutes.

Serves 4 to 6.

I've never tried cooking this dish in the oven. If anyone out there wants to try, let me know what you did and how it turns out!

MASHED COCO & CODFISH

Coco is also known as taro root and is readily available in West Indian and Asian markets, as well as in many large supermarkets. You can substitute eddoes or potatoes for coco.

1 lb coco, peeled
water to cover
¼ tsp salt
2 tbsp oil
2 tbsp onion, chopped
1 escallion, chopped
1 medium tomato, diced
1 lb prepared salt cod, flaked (see note on p. 17)
2 tbsp butter
salt and black pepper to taste
1 whole Scotch bonnet pepper, seeded and finely chopped

In a stockpot, boil cocos in salted water for 20 to 25 minutes
    until they are tender.
Remove coco and cool. Mash coarsely and set aside.
In a saucepan over medium heat, sauté onion, escallion, tomatoes,
    and cod in oil for 5 minutes.
Add coco, butter, salt, pepper, and hot pepper sauce and cook
    for 10 to 15 minutes, until flavors are blended.

Serves 4 to 6.

JERK SNAPPER STUFFED WITH CALLALOO

This stuffed fish will "snap" back at you with its jerk touch.

3 1-lb whole red snappers, scaled and cleaned

1 tbsp lime juice

3 cups water

1 tsp salt

1 tsp black pepper

4 tbsp jerk sauce (p. 20)

2 tsp olive oil

1 small onion, sliced

1 medium carrot, cut into strips

6 whole okra, cut in half, lengthwise

1 cup canned callaloo or 1½ cups of fresh spinach, chopped

4 tbsp butter

fresh lime wedges (garnish)

Preheat oven to 375°F, or barbecue to 350°F.

In a large bowl, wash fish with water and lime juice.

Season with salt, pepper and 1 tbsp of the jerk sauce. Set aside.

In a separate bowl, combine remaining jerk sauce,
 olive oil, onion, carrot, okra, and callaloo or spinach.

Stuff mixture into fish cavity. Dot each fish with 1 tbsp butter.

Lightly grease foil with olive oil or non-stick spray.

Wrap each fish in foil. Bake in the oven or on the barbecue
 for 20 to 30 minutes.

Serves 2 to 4.

STEAMED SNAPPER

3 1-lb red snappers, scaled and cleaned

1 tsp salt

1 tsp black pepper

1 medium onion, sliced

2 cloves garlic, sliced

1 large carrot, peeled and sliced

1 large tomato, chopped

1 small green pepper, sliced

6 okra, chopped or 1 8-oz pkg frozen

1 sprig fresh thyme

4 tbsp margarine

½ cup water

4 cups cabbage, roughly chopped

Season fish with salt and pepper.

In a large saucepan over medium heat, combine fish and all remaining
ingredients except cabbage, and cook for 5 minutes.

Lower heat, cover, and steam for 10 minutes, then add cabbage
and steam for another 5 minutes.

Transfer fish to platter and serve with vegetables on top.

Serves 4 to 6.

ESCOVITCHED SNAPPER

You can serve this dish hot or cold, with hard-dough bread (found in West Indian markets), Fried Dumplings (p. 139), or Bammy (p. 124).

6 1-lb snappers, scaled and cleaned
1 tbsp salt
1 tbsp black pepper
1 cup vegetable oil
1 large onion, sliced
¼ cup water
½ cup white vinegar
1 sprig fresh thyme, chopped

¼ tsp whole allspice seeds
2 whole Scotch bonnet peppers,
seeded and sliced (see note on p. 15)
1 medium carrot, sliced
½ medium green pepper, seeded
and sliced
½ medium red pepper, seeded
and sliced

Season fish with salt and pepper.

In a large, heavy saucepan over medium heat, fry fish in oil 5 to 10 minutes on each side, until golden brown.

Transfer fish to a serving dish.

Discard half the oil. In the remaining oil, sauté onions over low heat for 2 minutes.

Add remaining ingredients and let simmer for 5 minutes.

Serve over fish.

Serves 2-4.

JERK SALMON STEAKS

1 tbsp olive oil
¼ tsp black pepper
¼ tsp salt
1 tbsp jerk sauce (p. 20)

¼ tsp fresh thyme, chopped
¼ tsp lime juice
4 salmon steaks, ¾" thick
lime wedges (garnish)

In a large bowl, combine olive oil, salt, pepper, jerk sauce, thyme, and lime juice.

Add salmon and marinate for 30 minutes.

Preheat barbecue or grill to 375°F.

Grill salmon steaks for 7 to 10 minutes on each side.

Serve garnished with lime slices.

Serves 4.

SALMON STEAKS IN TAMARIND SAUCE

1 tbsp olive oil

¼ tsp salt

¼ tsp black pepper

¼ tsp lime juice

4 salmon steaks, ¾" thick

¼ cup tamarind dressing (p. 30)

fresh lime wedges (garnish)

In a large bowl, combine olive oil, salt, and pepper.

Add salmon and marinate for 30 minutes.

Preheat barbecue or grill to 375°F.

Grill salmon steaks for 7 to 10 minutes on each side.

Serve with Tamarind Dressing (p. 30) and lime wedges.

Serves 4.

JERK SWORDFISH

Swordfish has a coarse, firm texture and should be pricked with a fork before grilling. This will let you separate flakes when cooked.

4 tbsp olive oil

1 tsp lime juice

3 tbsp jerk sauce (p. 20)

1 tsp fresh thyme, chopped

¼ tsp dried basil

½ tsp salt

1 tsp black pepper

4 8-oz swordfish steaks

lemon wedges (garnish)

In a large bowl, combine olive oil, lime juice,
    jerk seasoning, thyme, basil, salt, and pepper.

Add fish and marinate for 30 minutes.

Preheat barbecue, or grill to 350°F.

Grill fish for 15 to 25 minutes, turning often.

Serve with lemon wedges.

Serves 4.

Swordfish can also be broiled in the oven, 8 to 10 minutes per side.

FRIED FLYING FISH

Flying fish is popular in Barbados and Tobago. Flying fish is readily available in West Indian and Asian markets, and in larger supermarkets. It comes in 1-pound packages, fresh or frozen, with about 5 small fish per pound. Try this recipe with Lemon & Lime Sauce (p. 25).

½ cup flour
¼ tsp salt
¼ tsp black pepper
1 tbsp fine, dry bread crumbs
1 1-lb pkg flying fish fillets
1 tbsp lime juice
1 tbsp garlic powder
1 tsp onion powder
¼ tsp fresh thyme, chopped
1 tbsp celery salt
black pepper to taste
1 egg
3 tbsp vegetable oil
lime wedges (garnish)
fresh parsley, finely copped (garnish)

In a medium bowl, combine flour, salt, pepper, and bread crumbs. Set aside.
In a separate bowl, wash fish with lime juice and water.
Drain, then season fish with garlic powder and onion powder, thyme,
    celery salt, and pepper. Set aside for 30 minutes.
Using a whisk, beat the egg.
Pour over fish, then coat fish with flour mixture.
In a saucepan over medium heat, fry fish in oil 5 to 8 minutes each side until
    nicely browned.
Drain fish on paper towels to absorb excess oil.
To serve, garnish with lime wedges and parsley.

Serves 2.

KINGFISH STEW

The next two recipes call for kingfish, but you can substitute grouper or red snapper.

6 slices kingfish, or 3 red snappers or groupers, filleted
¼ tsp salt
¼ tsp black pepper
1 cup vegetable oil
2 onions, sliced
2 stalks escallion, chopped
1 large tomato, chopped
¼ tsp salt
¼ tsp black pepper
¼ tsp ground allspice
1 sprig thyme, chopped
¼ tsp jerk sauce (p. 20)
1 cup water

Season fish with salt and pepper.

In a large, heavy saucepan over medium heat, fry fish in oil until lightly browned on both sides. Remove and set aside.

Discard half the oil. To the remaining oil, add the onions, tomato, salt, pepper, allspice, thyme, and jerk sauce and sauté for 2 minutes.

Add water and let simmer until flavors are blended, then add fish, lower heat, cover, and let simmer for another 10 minutes.

Serves 2 to 4.

STEWED FISH AT THE JERK

This recipe is another great kingfish dish from The Real Jerk. The jerk sauce is optional, but if you like extra heat, add it in.

8 slices kingfish or grouper
½ tsp salt
1 tsp black pepper
¼ cup flour
1 cup vegetable oil
1 large onion, chopped
1 medium green pepper, seeded and chopped
1 large tomato, chopped
1 small green pepper, seeded and chopped
1 sprig fresh thyme, chopped
1 tbsp white vinegar
1 Scotch bonnet pepper, seeded and chopped (see note on p. 15)
½ cup ketchup
¼ tsp ground allspice
1 tsp garlic powder
¼ cup water
1 tsp salt
1 tsp black pepper
½ tsp jerk sauce (p. 20) (optional)

Season fish with salt and pepper, then dust with flour.
In a large, heavy saucepan over medium heat, fry fish in oil until
    lightly brown on both sides.
Remove fish and set aside.
Discard oil, reserving ¼ cup for sauce.
In a medium saucepan, heat reserved oil.
Add onions, tomatoes, peppers, and thyme and sauté for 2 minutes.
Stir in vinegar, Scotch bonnet pepper, ketchup, allspice, garlic powder,
    water, salt, pepper, and jerk sauce and let simmer for 5 minutes.
Add fish, cover pot, and let simmer for another 10 minutes.

Serves 2 to 4.

CURRY FISH

This curry is best served simply, with steamed white rice. You can use any kind of white fish.

6 slices grouper
¼ tsp salt
¼ tsp pepper
½ cup flour
1 cup vegetable oil
1 medium onion, sliced
1 stalk escallion, chopped
6 whole pimento (allspice) berries
¼ tsp ground ginger
½ tsp garlic powder
2 tbsp curry powder
1 sprig thyme, chopped
salt and black pepper to taste
½ cup water

Season grouper with salt and pepper, then lightly dust with flour.
In a large, heavy saucepan over medium heat, fry fish in oil, 4 pieces
    at a time, for about 5 minutes each side, until lightly brown.
Drain, reserving ¼ cup oil. Set fish aside.
In the remaining oil, sauté onions, escallion, allspice berries, ginger,
    garlic and curry powders, thyme, salt, and pepper for 3 minutes.
Add water and fish.
Cover, lower heat, and let simmer for 10 minutes.
Remove allspice berries before serving.

Serves 4 to 6.

On our first cruise, one of our favorite pastimes was watching these lovely fish follow the lights of the ship. We didn't catch any, though!

Seafood

CURRY SHRIMP

2 tbsp flour

¼ cup water

3 tbsp olive oil

2 medium onions, sliced

2 cloves garlic, chopped

2 tbsp curry powder

1 lb medium shrimp, peeled and deveined

1 small green pepper, cut into strips

1 sprig fresh thyme, chopped

½ tsp salt

¼ tsp black pepper

In a small bowl, whisk together flour and water. Set aside.

In a large saucepan over medium heat, sauté onions, garlic,
and curry powder in oil for 2 minutes.

Add flour and water mixture and cook for another 2 minutes.

Stir in shrimp, green pepper, thyme, salt, and pepper and cook
for another 2 to 5 minutes or until shrimp turn pink.

Serves 4.

SHRIMP CREOLE

Served with steamed rice, Shrimp Creole makes a quick and easy dinner.

1 lb medium shrimp, peeled and deveined

¼ tsp salt

¼ tsp black pepper

½ tsp garlic powder

⅛ tsp ground allspice

3 tbsp vegetable oil

1 large onion, chopped in large pieces

2 medium tomatoes, chopped in large pieces

1 large green pepper, seeded and chopped in large pieces

1 tsp white vinegar

¼ cup ketchup

1 tsp sugar

½ tsp Scotch bonnet pepper, seeded and minced (see note on p. 15)

In a medium bowl, season shrimp with salt, pepper, garlic powder, and allspice.

In a large saucepan over medium heat, sauté onions and shrimp in oil for 2 to 3 minutes. Set aside.

In the same saucepan combine tomatoes, green peppers, vinegar, ketchup, sugar, and Scotch bonnet pepper and sauté for 5 to 7 minutes.

Add onions and shrimp and cook for an additional minute.

Serves 6.

SHRIMP CREOLE PASTA

1 medium tomato, chopped

½ small onion, sliced

2 tbsp vegetable oil

¼ small green pepper, sliced

1 sprig fresh thyme, chopped

24 medium shrimp, peeled and deveined

¼ cup ketchup

⅓ tsp jerk sauce (p. 20)

salt and black pepper to taste

1½ cup cooked penne pasta

In a large saucepan over medium heat, sauté tomatoes, onions, green peppers, and thyme in oil for 3 minutes.

Stir in shrimp, ketchup, jerk sauce, salt, and pepper and cook for another 2 minutes.

Add pasta and cook for 2 to 3 minutes.

Serves 2.

SHRIMP & CHICKEN PASTA

1 cup rundown sauce (p. 22)

12 Black tiger shrimp, peeled and deveined

1 6-oz cooked jerk chicken breast (p. 100), sliced

1 small tomato, chopped

1 sprig fresh thyme, chopped

1 small green pepper, sliced

salt and black pepper to taste

1½ cups cooked penne pasta

In a saucepan over medium heat, combine rundown sauce, shrimp, chicken, tomato, and thyme.

Let simmer for 3 minutes.

Add green pepper, salt, pepper, and pasta, and cook for 5 minutes, adding extra water if needed to make more sauce.

Serves 4.

COCONUT SHRIMP

This dish uses Black tiger shrimp, a warm-water shrimp with a dark blue shell and yellow stripes. Serve these hot with Tamarind Dressing (p. 30) or Mango Salsa (p. 28) as a main dish or as an appetizer.

½ cup flour
1 tsp baking powder
¼ tsp salt
¼ tsp pepper
1¼ cup beer
¼ cup flour (for dredging)
1 cup unsweetened coconut, fine or coarse
2 cups vegetable oil
24 Black tiger shrimp, peeled and deveined,
  leaving the tails on (see note on p. 17)

In a medium bowl, combine flour, baking powder, salt, and pepper.
Add beer and whisk until the batter has the smooth consistency
    of cake batter.
Place dredging flour and coconut in two separate, smaller bowls.
In a large, heave saucepan, heat oil to 360°F.
Dredge each shrimp in the flour, then in the batter.
Then roll in the coconut.
Deep-fry shrimp, in small batches, until they have curled and are
    a lovely golden color.

Serves 6 to 8.

PEPPER SHRIMP

These can be served hot or cold and make a great appetizer. If you like, you can leave the shells intact and peel as you eat. Try them with Zippy Dipping Sauce (p. 25).

2 tbsp olive oil
1 lb Black tiger shrimp or medium prawns, peeled and deveined, leaving tails on
2 Scotch bonnet peppers, non-seeded but sliced (see note on p. 15)
1 tbsp white vinegar
pinch of ground allspice
salt and black pepper to taste

In a large saucepan over medium heat, sauté shrimp until they are almost fully pink.
Add remaining ingredients and cook for another 2 minutes.

Serves 4 to 6.

JANGA PASTA

A Real Jerk twist on Italy's favorite starch. "Janga" is Jamaican for any kind of shrimp.

3 tbsp vegetable oil
12 medium Black tiger shrimp
1 cup Rundown Sauce (p. 22)
1 small tomato, chopped
1 medium green pepper, seeded and cut into strips
¼ tsp black pepper
¼ tsp salt
jerk sauce or hot pepper sauce to taste (optional)
1 cup cooked linguine or penne pasta

In a large saucepan over medium heat, combine all ingredients except pasta.
Let simmer for 5 minutes.
Add pasta and cook for another 5 minutes.

Serves 2.

JERKED AND BUTTERFLIED JUMBO SHRIMP

15 jumbo or Black tiger shrimp, butterflied (see note on p. 17)
3 tbsp olive oil
1 tbsp jerk sauce (p. 20)
¼ tsp cayenne pepper
3 lemon wedges

Preheat oven to 400°F.

Arrange shrimp on a greased baking sheet.

In a small bowl, combine olive oil, jerk sauce, and the juice from one of the wedges of lemon.

Brush shrimp with mixture, then sprinkle lightly with cayenne pepper.

Broil for 7 to 10 minutes.

Serve hot, garnished with remaining lemon wedges.

Serves 4 to 6.

JERK PRAWNS

A fiery appetizer, or an equally fiery main dish.

12 large Black tiger shrimp
¼ tsp salt
¼ tsp black pepper
1 tsp vegetable oil
1 tsp jerk sauce (p. 20)
lime wedges (garnish)

In a medium bowl, season shrimp with salt and pepper.

In a separate bowl, combine oil and jerk sauce. Pour over prawns.

Preheat barbecue or grill to 375°F.

Grill shrimp 7 minutes each side or until they are bright pink.

Serve garnished with lime wedges.

Serves 2.

SHRIMP, LENTIL & CHICKPEA CURRY

Serve this curry with steamed rice or in Roti shells (p. 131).

- **½ onion, chopped**
- **2 cloves garlic, chopped**
- **2 sprigs fresh thyme, whole**
- **1 whole Scotch bonnet pepper**
- **1 tsp onion powder**
- **2 tbsp curry powder**
- **½ tsp ground cumin**
- **½ tsp salt**
- **1 tsp black pepper**
- **3 tbsp vegetable oil**
- **1 cup water**
- **1 19 oz-can chickpeas, undrained**
- **1 8 oz-can green lentils**
- **½ lb shrimp, peeled and deveined**

In a large saucepan over medium heat, sauté onions, garlic, thyme, Scotch bonnet pepper, onion powder, curry powder, cumin, salt, and pepper in oil for 2 minutes, stirring frequently to blend ingredients.

Add water. Bring to a boil.

Add chickpeas and lentils.

Lower heat, cover, and let simmer for 5 to 8 minutes, stirring occasionally.

Add shrimp and cook another 2 to 5 minutes.

Remove sprigs of thyme and Scotch bonnet pepper before serving.

Serves 4.

SHRIMP FRIED RICE

You can buy dried shrimp in West Indian and Asian markets and in many large supermarkets.

1 cup dried shrimp
2 tbsp vegetable oil
1 small onion, chopped
1 stalk escallion, chopped
1 egg, beaten
2 tbsp margarine
3 cups cooked white rice
1 tsp black pepper
½ tsp paprika
2 strips bacon, cooked and crumbled

Rinse shrimp to remove excess salt. Set aside.
In a large saucepan over medium heat, sauté onions for 2 minutes.
Add shrimp and sauté for another 2 minutes.
Stir in beaten egg and cook for one minute, then add remaining
    ingredients and cook for another 5 minutes, stirring often.

Serves 2 to 4.

To make this dish a true one-pot meal, add 1 cup of cooked mixed vegetables along with the cooked rice.

MUSSELS IN COCONUT SAUCE

Serve these mussels with your favorite bread to mop up every last drop of the sauce.

- **1 lb mussels**
- **1 tbsp lime juice**
- **3 tbsp vegetable oil**
- **1 medium onion, chopped**
- **2 tbsp curry powder**
- **1½ cups coconut milk (p. 21)**
- **½ tsp salt**
- **½ tsp black pepper**
- **½ cup water**
- **1 sprig thyme, chopped**
- **1 stalk escallion, chopped**
- **2 cloves garlic, chopped**
- **1 medium plum tomato, peeled and chopped**
- **½ lb Black tiger shrimp, peeled and deveined (optional)**

To prepare mussels, place them in a bowl of cold water.

With a stiff brush, scrub shells to remove sand and dirt.

Discard water and any mussels with open shells.

Refill bowl with clean cold water and the mussels.

Add lime juice and set aside while you prepare the sauce.

In a large saucepan over medium heat, sauté onions in oil for 2 minutes.

Blend in curry powder, coconut milk, water, salt, and pepper.

Lower heat and let simmer for 8 to 10 minutes.

Return heat to medium, add the mussels and the remaining ingredients and cook for another 3 to 5 minutes.

Discard any unopened mussels.

Serves 4.

MUSSELS IN SPICY SAUCE

This main dish also makes a good appetizer.

1 lb mussels
1 tbsp lime juice
3 tbsp vegetable oil
1 medium onion, sliced
2 cloves garlic, chopped
1" piece of fresh ginger root, peeled and sliced
1 tsp fresh thyme, chopped
2 cups water
1 tbsp chives, chopped
½ tsp salt
½ tsp black pepper
12 whole pimentos
2 medium plum tomatoes, peeled and chopped
3 tbsp oyster sauce
¼ tsp jerk sauce (p. 20)

To prepare mussels, place them in a bowl of cold water.
With a stiff brush, scrub shells to remove sand and dirt.
Discard water and any mussels with open shells.
Refill bowl with clean cold water and the mussels.
Add lime juice and set aside while you prepare the sauce.
In a large saucepan over medium heat, sauté onions, garlic, ginger, and
     thyme in oil for 3 minutes. Add water, chives, salt, pepper, and pimentos.
Lower heat and let simmer for 5 minutes.
Add the mussels and remaining ingredients, and cook for 3 to 5 minutes.
Discard any mussels that do not open.

Serves 4 to 6.

SCALLOPS WITH GARLIC & TOMATOES

1½ lbs bay scallops

salt and black pepper to taste

¼ cup olive oil

⅓ cup escallion, chopped

1 tsp garlic, finely chopped

1 cup fresh plum tomatoes, peeled, seeded, and diced

1 tbsp red wine vinegar

4 tbsp fresh parsley, finely chopped (garnish)

⅓ tsp fresh thyme, finely chopped (garnish)

Rinse scallops to remove any sand.

Sprinkle with salt and pepper and set aside.

In a large saucepan over medium heat, sauté escallion, garlic,
and tomatoes in 2 tbsp of the olive oil.

Add vinegar and cook for two minutes.

In another saucepan, heat remaining oil over high heat.

Add scallops and sauté for 1 minute. (Do not brown, or else
they will be overcooked.)

Transfer scallops to warmed plates.

Spoon tomato sauce over top and garnish with parsley and thyme.

Serves 4 to 6.

Meat&Poultry

JERK PORK

Jerk Pork and Fried Dumplings (p. 139) is a perennial favorite in Jamaica. Serve both with Festival (p. 138), Roasted Breadfruit (p. 125), or hard-dough bread. In Jamaica, we add leftover Jerk Pork to Ackee & Codfish (p. 48) and serve this dish for breakfast. Really!

4 lb boneless pork shoulder roast

3 tbsp salt

1 tbsp black pepper

3 tbsp garlic powder

2 tbsp onion powder

½ tsp ground allspice

1 tbsp soy sauce

½ cup jerk sauce (p. 20)

Cut pork shoulder into two pieces.

Using a butcher knife, make cuts 1" apart and ⅛ to ¼ " deep.

This will help the marinade soak into the roast.

Place in a shallow pan.

In a bowl, combine remaining ingredients.

Rub sauce over pork.

Cover and refrigerate overnight.

Preheat barbecue to 300ºF.

Slow cook pork until meat is brown and tender, about 45 minutes to 1 hour
or until meat thermometer inserted into meat reaches 160°F.

To serve, cut pork into 1" cubes.

Serves 8 to 10.

You can pre-cook the pork in a 300°F oven for about 40 minutes, then transfer to the barbecue and grill long enough to give it that rich, brown barbecue color.

PORK LOIN IN GINGER SAUCE

The Spaniards introduced ginger to the Caribbean in the 16th century. We use it in many main dishes, desserts, and drinks.

1 tsp salt
½ tsp black pepper
1 tbsp soy sauce
1 2-lb pork loin roast, cubed into 1" pieces
½ cup flour (for dredging)
¼ cup vegetable oil
1 cup water
2 tbsp fresh ginger root, peeled and grated
1 tbsp flour
1 sprig fresh thyme, chopped
1 tbsp honey
1 cup pineapple chunks (optional)

In a large bowl, combine salt, pepper, and soy sauce.

Add pork cubes and marinate for 15 minutes.

Lightly dredge cubes in flour.

In a large saucepan over medium high heat, sear pork in oil, in small batches, until meat is lightly browned.

Strain meat, transfer to a warming plate, and set aside.

Pour off excess oil from the saucepan, then add water and ginger root.

Return pan to stove and stir in flour, thyme, and honey.

Let simmer for 3 minutes or until sauce is thick, but smooth.

Add pork and pineapple chunks and let simmer another 3 to 5 minutes.

Serves 4 to 6.

When you buy fresh ginger root, look for firmness and a uniform color. Once cut, ginger will keep in the refrigerator if wrapped in plastic or stored in an airtight container.

JERK PORK CHOPS

This jerk pork recipe combines Jamaican and Asian flavors.

2 tbsp vegetable oil
⅓ cup jerk sauce (p. 20)
1 tbsp plum sauce
2 tbsp hoisin sauce
½ tsp salt
1 tbsp sugar
½ tsp white vinegar
8 pork chops, ½" thick

In a large bowl, combine oil and seasonings.
Add chops, cover, and refrigerate for 3 hours.
Preheat barbecue to 350ºF.
Grill chops for 30 to 40 minutes, turning often.

Serves 8.

 To oven bake, preheat oven to 350ºF. Bake for 30 minutes. Turn on broiler and broil chops 5 minutes each side.

COOK-UP PORK CHOPS

Pork chops always make a quick and easy dinner. In Jamaica, we say, "Let's cook up some pork chops tonight," hence the name of this recipe.

4 pork chops, ½" thick
½ tsp salt
½ tsp black pepper
3 tbsp flour (for dredging)
⅓ cup vegetable oil
1 medium onion, chopped
2 cloves garlic, chopped
½ sweet pepper, chopped
½ tomato, chopped
½ tsp fresh ginger, peeled and grated
1 tsp fresh thyme, chopped
2 tbsp soy sauce
1 sachet (cube) chicken bouillon, dissolved in water
⅓ cup water

Season pork chops with salt and pepper, then lightly dredge in flour.
In a large saucepan over medium heat, fry chops 7 minutes each side,
    until lightly browned.
Add remaining ingredients.
Lower heat, cover, and let simmer for 20 to 30 minutes, or until meat
    is tender.

Serves 4.

BARBECUED JERK RIBS

2 racks pork side ribs

water to cover

1 tsp salt

1 tbsp black pepper

1 tbsp garlic powder

½ tsp white vinegar

1 tbsp dried thyme

¼ tsp ground allspice

1 cup jerk rib sauce (p. 24)

In a large saucepan or stockpot, cover ribs with water.

Add remaining ingredients, except for jerk rib sauce.

Cover and bring to a boil.

Reduce heat, and let simmer for 45 minutes until ribs
     are firm but tender.

Remove ribs from pot and set aside.

Preheat barbecue to 325°F.

Grill ribs for 15 minutes.

Baste with jerk rib sauce and grill for another 10 minutes,
     turning ribs often.

Serves 4 to 6.

You can pre-cook ribs, with barbecue sauce, in a 350° to 400°F oven for 10
minutes, then transfer to the barbecue and grill long enough to give ribs
that rich, brown barbecue color.

HONEY-GLAZED BABY BACK RIBS

3 to 4 lbs pork baby back ribs
water to cover
2 medium onions, chopped
4 cloves garlic
4 whole cloves
6 whole pimento (allspice) berries
1 tsp ginger powder
2 sprigs fresh thyme, chopped
1 tsp black pepper
1 tbsp paprika
1 tbsp salt
1 whole Scotch bonnet pepper

SAUCE:
2 tbsp flour
¼ cup pineapple juice
6 tbsp brown sugar
½ cup honey
2 tbsp lime juice

Preheat oven to 325°F.

In a large saucepan or stockpot over medium heat,
combine ribs and just enough water to cover.

Add onions, garlic, cloves, allspice, ginger powder, thyme,
pepper, paprika, salt, and Scotch bonnet pepper

Let simmer for 20 to 30 minutes.

Transfer ribs to roasting pan.

For sauce:

In a medium saucepan over low heat, combine flour and
pineapple juice until mixed.

Add brown sugar, honey, and lime juice and let simmer for
5 minutes until sauce thickens. Set aside.

Brush ribs generously with sauce. Bake for 25 to 35 minutes.

Serves 6 to 8.

To barbecue ribs, let simmer ribs in stockpot for 20 to 30 minutes. Transfer
to a barbecue pre-heated 300°F and grill for 15 to 20 minutes, turning and
basting often with sauce.

CRAZY RIBS

Why do I call these ribs "crazy"? I'm not sure, except that when Ed and his pals gather in the backyard on a hot summer day, and the cold Red Stripe beer comes out, only "crazy" ribs will do. –L.

2 lbs pork riblets, cut into 1" pieces
1½ tbsp salt
1½ tbsp black pepper
3 tbsp jerk rib sauce (p. 24)
2 tbsp ketchup
1 tbsp soy sauce
2 tsp white vinegar
1 cup vegetable oil
juice of 1 lemon

Chop ribs between the bones and season with salt and pepper.

In a saucepan over medium heat, combine jerk rib sauce, ketchup, soy sauce, and vinegar and bring to a boil. Reduce heat and let simmer.

In another saucepan over medium heat, fry ribs in oil until they are brown and crispy.

Add ribs to sauce, ensuring each piece is well coated.

Transfer ribs to a serving plate and squeeze lemon over them.

Serves 4 to 6.

HOLIDAY HAM

As the name suggests, this ham recipe is perfect for special occasions.

1 8-10 lb picnic shoulder ham
enough water to cover
6 pimento (all-spice) berries
1 small onion, peeled
2 cloves garlic, chopped
1 sprig thyme
1 tbsp ginger, grated
6 whole cloves

SAUCE:
¼ cup orange juice
¼ cup pineapple juice
1 tsp lime juice
2 tbsp brown sugar
2 tbsp honey
1 whole clove

For sauce:

In a small bowl, combine the orange juice, pineapple juice, brown sugar, honey, and clove. Set aside.

Preheat oven to 350°F.

In a large stockpot, combine ham with the rest of the ingredients
and bring to a boil.

Lower heat and let simmer for 15 minutes.

Let cool, then remove ham from pot.

Peel skin and cut away the top layer of fat.

Using a paring knife, gently cut the top of ham in diagonal patterns
to form diamond shapes.

Place a clove at the corner of each diamond.

Place ham into an ovenproof dish and spoon sauce over it.

Bake in oven, basting every 10 minutes with remaining sauce,
until it is light brown in color, about 20-25 minutes.

STEWED BEEF

A flavorful stew with a hint of spice.

2 lbs stewing beef
1 tsp salt
1 tsp black pepper
3 tbsp vegetable oil
¼ cup water
2 medium potatoes, peeled and cut into chunks
1 medium carrot, chopped
1 large onion, chopped
3 cloves garlic, chopped
1 sprig fresh thyme, chopped
1 small green pepper, chopped
2 tbsp soy sauce
2 tbsp ketchup
¼ tsp paprika
1 sachet (cube) beef bouillon, dissolved in 1 cup water

Season beef with salt and pepper.

In a large saucepan over medium heat, brown beef in oil for 5 minutes.

Lower heat and add water. Cover and let steam for 20 minutes.

Add remaining ingredients, mixing well, then cook for another 45 minutes or
until meat is tender, adding extra water if needed for more gravy.

Serves 4 to 6.

CURRY BEEF

Curry beef can be served on its own or wrapped in a Roti shell (p. 131). The jerk sauce adds extra heat to this dish, but can be omitted if desired.

2 lbs stewing beef
1 tsp salt
1 tbsp black pepper
4 tbsp curry powder
2 tbsp vegetable oil
1 to 1½ cups water
1 large onion, chopped
2 medium potatoes, peeled quartered
2 medium carrots, peeled and chopped
1 sprig fresh thyme, chopped
2 cloves garlic, chopped
¼ tsp jerk sauce (p. 20) (optional)

In a large bowl, season beef with salt, pepper, and curry powder.
Cover and refrigerate for 1 hour.
In a large saucepan over medium heat, brown beef in oil for 10 minutes.
Add ½ cup water, lower heat, cover, and let simmer for another 30 minutes.
Stir in potatoes, carrots, and another ½ cup water.
Cover and cook for 45 minutes or until meat is tender, adding extra water
    if needed for more gravy.

Serves 4 to 6.

STEAK JAMAICAN STYLE

3 tbsp olive oil

2 cloves garlic, chopped

2 tbsp soy sauce

1 tsp onion powder

1 tsp black pepper

½ tsp salt

½ tsp ketchup

1 tsp Pikappeppa sauce or HP sauce

1 tsp fresh thyme, chopped

1 10-oz sirloin or T-bone steak

In a bowl, combine all ingredients except steak.

Add steak and marinate for at least 20 minutes.

Preheat barbecue to 350°F.

Barbecue steak for 7 minutes on both sides.

Serves 2.

Pikappeppa sauce can be found in most large supermarkets. There are various brands and various ways they spell the name: Pik-a-pepper, Pickapepper, or Pikappeppa. They're all the same tasty sauce.

JAMAICAN POT ROAST

Growing up in Jamaica, having pot roast was a treat; roasts were not often affordable for large, low-income families. Pot roast was cooked in a Dutch pot oven on a coal stove and it was usually served with Rice & Peas (p. 118) and a salad.

3 tsp salt
1 tsp black pepper
1 sprig fresh thyme, chopped
2 cloves garlic, chopped
2 stalks escallion, chopped
1 large onion, sliced
3 tbsp vegetable oil
1 bay leaf
1 tbsp soy sauce
4-5 lb pot roast (e.g., cross rib or blade roast)
1 cup water

In a large bowl, combine all ingredients except roast and water.

Add roast and marinate overnight in the refrigerator.

In a Dutch oven, brown roast in oil for 20 minutes, making sure to brown all sides evenly.

Lower heat, add water, cover, and let simmer for 1½ to 2 hours, until cooked or until a fork inserted into roast comes out clean.

Add extra water for more gravy.

Remove roast from pot and let sit for at least 15 minutes.

To serve, slice roast and pour gravy over top.

Serves 6 to 8.

AUNTIE P'S MINCEMEAT PASTA

Auntie P has been a cook with us at The Real Jerk for 14 years. Every once in awhile, she makes her mincemeat pasta just for the staff. We sit around the kitchen and enjoy this special dish with a salad and bread. It's our pleasure to share this recipe with you.

1 lb lean ground beef
1 medium onion, chopped
3 cloves garlic, chopped
¼ tsp salt
1 tsp black pepper
1 tbsp garlic powder
1 tsp fresh thyme, chopped
1 tbsp soy sauce
1 tsp paprika
3 tbsp vegetable oil
1 cup mixed vegetables
1 tbsp ketchup
½ cup water
1 cup cooked tri-color fusilli pasta

In a large bowl, combine ground beef, onion, garlic, salt,
    pepper, garlic powder, thyme, soy sauce, and paprika.
Let sit for 20 minutes.
In a large saucepan over medium heat, brown marinated
    beef in oil for 10 minutes.
Add water, ketchup, and mixed vegetables.
Lower heat, cover, and let simmer for 10 to 15 minutes,
    or until vegetables are cooked.
Remove pot from stove.
Spoon off excess oil, if necessary.
Add pasta and cook for another 5 minutes.

Serves 4.

CORNED BEEF MASH

Corned beef makes a quick and inexpensive meal. It was known in Jamaica as "Poor Man's Food" or "Bully Beef" after the most common brand imported to Jamaica from England.

1 14-oz can corned beef
¼ tsp black pepper
1 tsp onion, finely chopped
½ tsp hot pepper sauce

In a large bowl, mash corned beef with a fork.
Add remaining ingredients.
Serve as an appetizer on large crackers, topped with tomatoes,
    or as a main dish served over rice.

Serves 4.

 Ed's favorite sandwich is made with corned beef, onions, hot peppers, and tomatoes.

CORNED BEEF-STUFFED PASTA

These two recipes combine corned beef and pasta.

1 cup cooked jumbo pasta shells

1 19-oz can corned beef

3 tbsp tomatoes, finely chopped

1 tsp onion, finely chopped

2 tbsp vegetable oil

3 tbsp ketchup

½ tsp hot pepper sauce

½ tsp black pepper

In a large bowl, lightly oil cooked pasta shells and set aside.

In a separate bowl, combine all other ingredients.

Fill pasta shells with mixture and serve.

CORNED BEEF DELIGHT

1 large onion, sliced

1 medium tomato, chopped

1 tsp vegetable oil

1 19-oz can corned beef

¼ tsp black pepper

2 tbsp ketchup

2 cups cooked elbow macaroni

In a large saucepan over medium heat, sauté onions
and tomato in oil for two minutes.

Add corned beef, pepper, and ketchup, and macaroni,
and cook for another 2 minutes.

Both recipes serve 2 to 4.

CORNED BEEF OMELET

1 tsp milk
2 eggs, lightly beaten
dash each of salt and black pepper
½ onion, sliced
½ small tomato, chopped
2 tbsp vegetable oil
½ 19-oz can corned beef, softened with fork
1 tsp ketchup
½ tsp black pepper
dash of hot pepper sauce (optional)
2 tbsp vegetable oil (for eggs)

In a bowl, combine milk, beaten eggs, salt, and pepper and set aside.

In a saucepan over medium heat, sauté onions and tomatoes in oil
    for 2 minutes.

Add corned beef, ketchup, black pepper, and hot pepper sauce.

Let simmer for 3 minutes. Set aside.

In another saucepan, heat oil for eggs.

Pour in egg mixture to cover bottom of saucepan.

Cook until just firm.

Add corned beef mixture to one half of omelet, then fold over other half.

Serves 1 to 2.

STEWED KIDNEYS

In Jamaica, kidneys are usually eaten for breakfast with Boiled Bananas (p. 126) or Fried Dumplings (p. 139).

1½ lbs beef kidneys
½ tsp salt
1 tsp black pepper
1 tsp garlic powder
1 tsp onion powder
6 tbsp vegetable oil
1 medium onion, sliced
2 stalks escallion, chopped
1 sprig fresh thyme, chopped
1 medium tomato, chopped
½ green pepper, cut in strips
1 tbsp Pikappeppa sauce
2 tbsp ketchup
1 tbsp flour
1 tbsp butter
1 Scotch bonnet pepper, seeded and sliced (see note on p. 15)
1 cup water

Wash, skin, and cut away excess fat from kidneys.

Cut into medium-sized chunks.

Season with salt, pepper, and garlic and onion powders.

In a large saucepan over medium heat, brown kidneys
    in oil for 5 to 8 minutes.

Remove kidneys from pan and set aside.

Lower heat and sauté onions, escallion, thyme, tomatoes,
    and green pepper for 3 minutes.

Add Pikappeppa sauce, ketchup, flour, butter, Scotch bonnet
    pepper, and water, and let simmer for 2 minutes.

Return kidneys to saucepan, cover, and let simmer for another
    10 to 15 minutes.

Serves 6.

CURRY GOAT

Curry Goat is one of Jamaica's most popular dishes. Traditionally, it is prepared on special occasions, such as weddings, family gatherings, and holidays. At The Real Jerk, Curry Goat was not always well received by our customers; it took some hard work to convince them to "Go for it." Now they find it hard to resist! We serve it with steamed rice, Rice & Peas (p. 118), or as filling for Rotis (p. 131).

2 lbs goat meat, cubed
1 tbsp salt
1 tbsp black pepper
3 cloves garlic, chopped
1 tsp garlic powder
4 tbsp curry powder
1 stalk escallion, chopped

2 tbsp vegetable oil
2 cups water
2 medium onions, chopped
1 large potato, diced
3 sprigs fresh thyme, chopped
1 Scotch bonnet pepper, seeded
and chopped (see note on p. 15)

In a large bowl, combine salt, pepper, garlic, garlic powder, curry powder, and escallion.

Add goat meat and marinate for 30 minutes.

In a large saucepan over medium heat, brown goat meat in oil for 10 minutes.

Lower heat, cover pot, and allow meat to cook in its own juices for 10 minutes.

Add water and remaining ingredients and let simmer for 1 to 1½ hours, or until meat is tender.

Serves 6 to 8.

THE MISSING TOOTH, or
HOW LILY ALMOST GAVE AWAY THE REAL JERK

Over the years as a restaurant owner, you get into a number of interesting situations. One afternoon, a table of two women and one man were enjoying their meals. Suddenly, their server, visibly shaken, came to me and said that the male customer had a complaint. He had found what he believed to be a tooth in his curry goat. Now, curry goat is, by nature, quite bony, which I told him; but the customer, who was a dentist, argued that he knew a tooth when he saw one. I took the dentist's plate back to the kitchen and asked the staff if anyone had lost a tooth. No one had. I was just about to hand the dentist the keys to the restaurant when he came running into the kitchen, apologizing profusely. Apparently, he'd been enjoying his goat so much that he hadn't noticed that a tooth from his dentures had fallen out. –L.

STEWED OXTAIL

Not everyone's pleasure, but give it a try! It's a wonderfully rich meal.

2½ lbs oxtails, cut into ½" pieces
1 tbsp salt
1 tbsp black pepper
½ tsp paprika
3 tbsp vegetable oil
3 cloves garlic, chopped
1 large onion, chopped
2 tbsp fresh thyme, chopped
1½ cups water
2 tbsp soy sauce
2 tbsp ketchup
¼ tsp jerk sauce (p. 20) (optional)
1 14-oz can lima beans
10 to 12 spinners (p. 140) (optional)

In a large bowl, season oxtail with salt, pepper, and paprika.

In a large saucepan over medium heat, brown oxtails in oil for 15 minutes.

Add garlic, onion, and thyme and sauté for another 2 minutes.

Lower heat, add ½ cup water, cover, and let simmer for 45 minutes to
    1 hour, stirring often and adding remaining water when needed.

Stir in remaining ingredients and cook another 10 minutes.

Serves 4 to 6.

Stewed Chicken, p. 104

Curry Goat, p. 95 with **Fried Plantain**, p. 123

Stewed Oxtail, p. 96 with **Tangy Coleslaw**, p. 44
and **Rice & Peas**, p. 118

Curried Shrimp, p. 66

STEWED COW'S FOOT

Don't be squeamish now! This dish is a real Jamaican, and a Real Jerk, treat.

3 lbs cow's foot, sliced
6 cups water
2 cloves garlic, chopped
6 whole cloves
6 whole pimento (allspice) berries
1 tbsp salt
1 tbsp black pepper
2 medium onions, chopped
2 sprigs fresh thyme, chopped
2 stalks escallion, chopped
½ tsp Worcestershire sauce
3 tbsp olive oil
2 tbsp soy sauce
1 tsp onion powder
1 tbsp black pepper
½ tsp ketchup
1 tsp jerk sauce (p. 20)
3 sprigs fresh thyme, chopped
24 spinners

Wash cow's foot and, with a stiff brush, remove any hairs or rough spots.
In a large saucepan over medium heat, combine cow's foot, water, garlic, cloves, allspice, salt, and pepper.
Cover and let simmer for 1½ hours until cow's foot is tender.
Add all remaining ingredients.
Lower heat, cover, and let simmer another 15 minutes.

Serves 6 to 8.

Ask your butcher for "roasted" cow's foot. Not a must, but preferred!

JERK MEATBALLS

1 lb ground beef
1 small onion, finely chopped
¼ cup breadcrumbs
2 tbsp jerk sauce (p. 20)
1 tbsp garlic powder
1 egg
1 stalk escallion, finely chopped
1 tbsp soy sauce

Preheat oven to 350°F.
In a large bowl, combine all ingredients.
Roll into 2" round balls.
Bake on a greased baking sheet for 20 minutes.

Serves 4 to 6.

JERK LAMB CHOPS

A quick and easy recipe. Serve with good, old-fashioned mashed potatoes and your favorite steamed vegetables.

8 lamb chops, ½" inch thick
1 tsp jerk sauce (p. 20)
1 clove garlic, chopped
1 sprig fresh thyme, chopped
3 tbsp olive oil
salt and black pepper to taste

In a large baking dish, season chops with all ingredients.
Cover and marinate in the refrigerator for 1 hour.
Preheat oven to 400°F or barbecue to 375°F.
On a greased baking pan, bake chops for 10 minutes.
Turn on broiler and broil chops 3 to 5 minutes each side.
On a barbecue, grill chops 10 minutes each side.

Serves 6.

JERK CHICKEN

Jerk Chicken is a classic Jamaican dish, especially when served with hard-dough bread, Fried Dumplings (p. 139), Festival (p. 138), Roasted Breadfruit (p. 125) or Rice & Peas (p. 118).

3 lb chicken, cleaned and quartered (see note on p. 15)
1 tsp salt
½ tsp black pepper
½ tsp paprika
4 tbsp jerk sauce (p. 20)

Using a small knife, make two slits in each chicken quarter.
Season with salt, pepper, paprika, and jerk sauce.
Cover and marinate in the refrigerator for at least 1 hour or even overnight.
Preheat oven to 375°F and barbecue to 350°F .
Place chicken in a roasting pan and cook in the oven for 30 minutes.
Then transfer chicken to the barbecue and grill, turning chicken often,
     until it is cooked through.

Serves 6.

JERK CHICKEN WITH A BANG
In the early days of The Real Jerk, we did all the cooking. One day, I was alone in the restaurant, making my daily preparations, when I heard someone banging on the front door. When I went to investigate, I saw a young man, holding a briefcase, begging to be let in to eat some of our Jerk Chicken. Because it was two to three hours before opening, I didn't let him in. The banging continued. About fifteen minutes before opening I went back to the door to tell him to hang on. As I did, six police officers approached, their guns drawn. The man then pulled his own gun out of his briefcase, but the police were able to apprehend him before he was able to use it. In my shock and surprise, I asked if it was a real gun, to which one of the police officers replied: "It ain't jerk chicken." To this day, Ed and I often say, "Some people will do anything for Jerk Chicken." –L.

JERK CORNISH HENS

3 tbsp olive oil

1 tbsp chili seasoning

4 tbsp jerk sauce (p. 20)

½ tsp fresh thyme, chopped

¼ tsp salt

1 tsp black pepper

2 cloves garlic, chopped

2 Cornish hens

In a bowl, combine oil and all seasonings.

Add hens, cover, and refrigerate for at least 1 hour.

Preheat barbecue to 350°F.

Grill hens for about 45 minutes, turning often.

Serves 2.

To oven bake, place Cornish hens in a casserole dish and roast at 350°F for 1 hour. Baste hens at least twice during roasting.

JERK CHICKEN BREASTS

Great for sandwiches or as a salad topping!

3 boneless chicken breasts

3 tbsp vegetable oil

1 tsp salt

½ tsp onion powder

1 tbsp paprika

4 tbsp jerk sauce

In a large baking dish, season chicken with oil and all seasonings.

Cover and marinate in the refrigerator for 30 minutes.

Preheat oven or barbecue to 350ºF.

On the barbecue, grill chicken for 20 to 30 minutes, or until chicken is cooked. In the oven, bake chicken for 30 minutes, or until cooked.

Serves 2 to 4.

JERK CHICKEN WRAP

These wraps make a great lunch or a light supper. They can be served cold or warmed in a microwave.

½ **small avocado**
3 vegetable wraps (or tortilla shells)
3 6-oz-cooked jerk chicken breasts (p. 100), cut in strips
1 small tomato, finely chopped
½ **cup lettuce, finely shredded**
salt and black pepper to taste

Cut avocado in half.
Scoop out flesh, mash with a fork, then spread on wraps or tortilla shells.
Add strips of chicken. Top with tomatoes and lettuce.
Sprinkle with salt and pepper. Wrap.

Serves 4 to 6.

JERK CHICKEN PASTA IN RUNDOWN SAUCE

This dish, also known as "Couby," is a specialty at the Real Jerk. The rundown sauce gives this quick and easy-to-prepare dish its unique flavor. We've listed the jerk sauce as optional, but it does give this dish an extra bit of heat.

**1 boneless chicken breast,
  cut in strips**
½ **cup rundown sauce (p. 22)**
1 small tomato, chopped
**1 medium green pepper,
  cut in strips**

¼ **tsp salt**
¼ **tsp black pepper**
½ **tsp jerk sauce (p. 20) (optional)**
**1 cup cooked linguine or
  penne pasta**

In a large saucepan over medium heat, combine all ingredients except pasta. Cover and let simmer for 5 minutes.
Add cooked pasta and let simmer for another 5 minutes, stirring often.

Serves 2.

JERK WINGS

Served with a cold bottle of Red Stripe beer, these wings are great for a Sunday afternoon picnic.

1 tbsp vegetable oil
2 tbsp jerk sauce
1 tbsp barbecue sauce
2 lbs chicken wings, tips removed

In a large bowl, combine oil, jerk sauce, and barbecue sauce.
Add wings, cover, and marinate in the refrigerator for at least 20 minutes.
Preheat barbecue to 375°F.
Grill wings for 30-40 minutes, or until well done.

Serves 4 to 6.

ISLAND PIZZA

Did you think that only Italy had the goods on great pizza? Think again!

1 medium avocado
1 tbsp olive oil
1 tsp lime juice
4 large tortilla shells
1 small onion, chopped
1 small green pepper, chopped
1 small tomato, chopped
1 8 oz jerk chicken breast (p. 100), cooked and diced
½ cup marble cheese, coarsely grated

Preheat oven to 350ºF.
Peel and halve avocado. Remove pit and spoon out flesh.
In a bowl, combine avocado flesh, olive oil, and lime juice.
Spread mixture on tortillas, then top with remaining ingredients.
Bake tortillas on a greased cookie sheet or pizza pan for 15 minutes, until
    tortillas are lightly brown and crispy, and the cheese has melted.

Serves 4.

JA FRIED CHICKEN

Zippy Dipping Sauce (p. 25) makes a tasty condiment for this dish.

4 chicken drumsticks	**1 tsp salt**
2 chicken breasts, cut in half	**1 tsp black pepper**
1 tbsp garlic powder	**1 cup milk**
¼ tsp ginger powder	**½ cup flour**
½ tsp paprika	**2 cups vegetable oil for deep frying**

In a large bowl, season chicken drumsticks and breasts with garlic and ginger powders, paprika, salt, and pepper.

Cover and refrigerate for 1 hour.

Pour milk over chicken breasts, let stand for 10 minutes, then dredge in flour.

In a large, heavy saucepan or deep-fryer, heat oil to 360°F.

Deep-fry chicken, 4 pieces at a time, until golden.

Serves 4 to 6.

GOLDEN FRIED CHICKEN

Move over, Colonel Saunders! The Real Jerk recipe for fried chicken is second to none.

3 chicken breasts, cut in half	**½ cup flour**
1 tsp salt	**¼ cup cornmeal**
1 tsp black pepper	**¼ tsp salt**
½ tsp paprika	**¼ tsp black pepper**
1 egg yolk	**2 cups vegetable oil**
2 tbsp milk	

In a large bowl, season chicken with salt, pepper, and paprika.

In a separate bowl, beat egg yolk and milk together then pour over chicken, making sure that each piece is well covered.

In another bowl, combine flour, cornmeal, salt, and pepper.

In a deep-fryer or large, heavy saucepan, heat oil to 360°F.

Dredge each piece of chicken in flour and cornmeal mixture, then deep-fry, 4 pieces at a time, until golden.

Serves 4 to 6.

STEWED CHICKEN

Stewed chicken, served with rice and peas and a salad, is a tradition in many Jamaican homes. Sundays without this main dish just wouldn't be Sunday! There is only one thing you should know about stewed chicken: the method of cooking varies from home to home. But this is a great one to try!

1 whole chicken, cut up
¼ tsp salt
¼ tsp black pepper
1 cup vegetable oil

FOR SAUCE:
2 cloves garlic
1 medium onion, chopped
1 small tomato, chopped
¼ cup red pepper, chopped
1 sprig thyme
1 tbsp soy sauce
¼ tsp all-spice powder (optional)
2 cups water or chicken stock
2 tbsp flour

Wash the chicken pieces, then season with salt and pepper.

In a pot over high heat, fry the chicken pieces in oil, no more than 4 pieces at a time, until light brown on both sides. Set aside.

Discard half of the oil, lower heat to medium, and add garlic, onion, tomato, thyme, soy sauce, and all-spice powder.

Sauté for 5 minutes, then mix in flour and continue cooking for 1 minute, stirring often.

Add water or chicken stock, and stir.

Return chicken pieces to pot and cover.

Simmer until chicken is fully cooked, approximately 15 minutes.

CURRY CHICKEN

Curry Chicken is one of Jamaica's best-loved dishes. One of my fondest school memories is eating curry chicken with Fried Dumplings (p. 139) and Boiled Bananas (p. 126) at end-of-school parties on sandy, white beaches. During these times, I would think to myself, "Life could never be any better!" –L.

2 lbs boneless chicken thighs, cubed
2 medium white potatoes, peeled and cut into chunks
1 large carrot, chopped
2 medium onions, chopped
2 cloves garlic, chopped
3 tsp fresh thyme, chopped
3 tbsp curry powder
1 tsp salt
1 tsp black pepper
¼ tsp pimento (allspice) berries
1 Scotch bonnet pepper, seeded and sliced (optional) (see note on p. 15)
½ tsp jerk sauce (p. 20) (optional)
3 tbsp vegetable oil
½ cup water or chicken stock (p. 32)
½ small green pepper, chopped

In a large bowl, combine all the ingredients except oil, water, and green pepper.
Cover and marinate in the refrigerator for 30 minutes.
In a large, covered saucepan over medium heat, cook chicken in oil for 15 minutes.
Add water or chicken stock, reduce heat, and let simmer for 20 minutes, until chicken is tender.
Stir in green peppers and serve.

Serves 6

There are many other vegetables that you could add to this dish, such as celery root and cho cho, or your own favorites.

JERK TURKEY

Surprise your Christmas dinner guests with this spicy variation on the holiday bird. Brining the turkey first in salt, lime juice, and water will make it juicier and more flavorful.

- **1 12-lb turkey**
- **4 tbsp salt**
- **1 tbsp lime juice**
- **enough water to cover turkey**
- **1 tbsp back pepper**
- **4 cloves, garlic, minced**
- **2 tbsp onion powder**
- **1 tsp ginger powder**
- **1 tsp paprika**
- **2 sprigs thyme, chopped**
- **4 tbsp jerk sauce (p. 20)**
- **4 tbsp vegetable oil**
- **¼ cup soy sauce**
- **4 tbsp butter**

In a large container, place turkey, salt, water, and lime juice, then cover and keep in the refrigerator for at least two hours.

In a small bowl, combine the pepper, garlic, onion powder, ginger powder, paprika, thyme, Jerk Sauce, oil, and soy sauce to form a paste.

Remove turkey from refrigerator and discard the salt water mixture.

Place turkey in a roasting pan and season with spice mixture, rubbing on outside and inner cavity of turkey, then cover and refrigerate for at least 1 hour.

Let turkey come back to room temperature after removing from refrigerator again.

Preheat oven to 350°F.

Dot turkey with butter, then cover roasting pan and place in oven to roast for 1 hour.

Remove cover and baste turkey with dripping from the turkey pan, then continue roasting until turkey reaches an internal temperature of 170°F (use a meat thermometer).

Side Dishes

STEAMED CALLALOO

Callaloo is a dark green, leafy vegetable rich in iron. Substitutions include spinach or Swiss chard, but if you have a West Indian market near you, buy the real thing. There's no other vegetable that tastes just like it. If fresh callaloo isn't available, ask for canned. Callaloo can be served with Fried Dumplings (p. 139), steamed rice, bread, or as a filling for Roti shells (p. 131).

1 large onion, sliced

1 tbsp vegetable oil

⅓ cup water

1 14- oz can callaloo, or 2 cups fresh, chopped

1 large tomato, sliced

1 tbsp margarine

¼ tsp salt

½ tsp black pepper

In a large saucepan over medium heat, sauté onions in oil until they are opaque. Add remaining ingredients.

Lower heat, cover, and steam for 15 minutes.

When using fresh callaloo, cook for 20 minutes.

Serves 2 to 4.

To prepare fresh callaloo: strip and cut away the stalks, buds, and dried leaves. Wash the fresh leaves before chopping. It can be served several different ways depending on the time of the day. For breakfast, add pieces of bacon; for lunch or dinner, add sliced carrots, cho cho, or Steamed Cabbage (p. 121).

CALLALOO FRITTERS

1 14-oz can callaloo, or
  2 cups fresh, chopped
1 small onion, chopped
1 small tomato, chopped
1 tbsp margarine, melted
½ cup water

1 large egg, beaten
1½ cups flour
1 tbsp baking powder
¼ tsp salt
¼ tsp black pepper
½ cup vegetable oil

In a large saucepan over low heat, combine callaloo, onion, tomato,
    melted margarine, and water. Cover and steam for 10 minutes.
Set aside and cool, then add beaten egg.
In a large bowl, combine flour, baking powder, salt, and pepper.
Stir in callaloo mixture to form a batter, adding water if the batter is too stiff.
In a large, heavy saucepan or deep-fryer, heat oil to 360°F.
Drop tablespoons of batter, 4 at a time, into oil and deep-fry until golden.

Serves 4 to 6.

CALLALOO RICE

3 cups water
1 14-oz can of callaloo, or 2 cups fresh, chopped
2 tbsp margarine
1 small onion, chopped
1 cup coconut milk (p. 21)
1 tsp salt
¼ tsp black pepper
1½ cups uncooked white rice

In a large saucepan, bring water to boil.
Add all ingredients except rice. Boil for 10 minutes.
Lower heat, stir in rice, cover, and steam for 20 minutes.

Serves 4 to 6.

CURRY LENTILS

Rastafarians are vegetarians. They eat what is called "ital" foods, meaning natural or organic. I discovered this great vegetarian dish at Reggae Beach in Ocho Rios. At the restaurant, I serve it with steamed rice or as a filling for Rotis (p. 131). –L.

2 tbsp vegetable oil
1 medium onion
2 cloves garlic, chopped
1 tbsp curry powder
½ cup coconut milk (p. 21)
½ cup okra, sliced
½ cup pumpkin, chopped
¼ cup carrot, diced
1 19-oz can green lentils
⅓ cup milk
½ tsp salt
½ tsp black pepper

In a saucepan over medium heat, sauté onions, garlic, and curry powder in oil for 1 minute.

Stir in coconut milk, okra, pumpkin, and carrots and cook for 5 minutes.

Add remaining ingredients, lower heat, cover pot, and let simmer for another 10 minutes.

Serves 4 to 6.

LENTIL RICE

1 19-oz can lentils	¼ tbsp salt
1 cup coconut milk (p. 21)	1 tsp black pepper
1 small onion, chopped	1 tsp garlic powder
1 sprig fresh thyme, chopped	2 tbsp margarine
1 stalk escallion, chopped	3 cups uncooked white rice

In a large saucepan over high heat, combine all ingredients except rice.
Boil for 10 minutes. Lower heat, stir in rice, cover, and steam for 25 minutes.

Serves 4 to 6.

CURRY POTATOES

Curry potatoes makes a good accompaniment to your favorite curry meat, fish, or chicken dish. It's also good on its own or wrapped in a Roti (p. 131). For extra heat, add the hot pepper sauce.

4 tbsp vegetable oil
1 lb potatoes, peeled and cubed
3 tbsp curry powder
¼ tsp ground cumin
¼ tsp salt
¼ tsp black pepper
1 tbsp garlic powder
1 tbsp onion powder
1 sprig fresh thyme, chopped (optional)
hot pepper sauce to taste (optional)
1 cup water

In a large saucepan over medium heat, combine potatoes and
    seasonings until potatoes are well coated.
Add water, cover, and let simmer until potatoes are tender.

Serves 3 to 4.

MASHED PUMPKIN & POTATO

6 cups water

½ tsp salt

1 lb white potatoes, peeled and diced

½ lb pumpkin, peeled, seeded, and diced

4 tbsp butter

¼ cup evaporated milk

⅓ cup milk (optional)

In a large saucepan over medium heat, bring water to boil.

Add salt and potatoes and cook for 5 minutes.

Add pumpkin and cook for another 15 minutes, or until potatoes
and pumpkin are tender.

Strain and mash, adding in butter, evaporated milk, and regular milk,
if desired.

Serves 4 to 6.

SWEET POTATO BALLS

4 cups water
¼ tsp salt
1 lb sweet potatoes, peeled and cubed
1 egg
¼ cup breadcrumbs
¼ tsp cinnamon
1 tbsp sugar
1 tbsp vegetable oil
1 cup vegetable (for frying)

In a large saucepan over medium heat, bring water to boil.

Add salt and sweet potatoes, and cook for 20 minutes, or until potatoes are tender.

Strain potatoes and cool, then mash, adding in egg, breadcrumbs, cinnamon, sugar, and vegetable oil.

Roll mixture into 2" round balls.

In medium saucepan over medium heat, fry balls in oil until lightly browned.

Place on paper towels to absorb excess oil.

Serves 4.

To bake in the oven, preheat oven to 400°F. Place balls on greased baking sheet and bake for 20 minutes.

GOONGO PEA STEW

2 tbsp vegetable oil

1 small onion, finely chopped

2 stalks escallion, chopped

2 cloves garlic, chopped

3 tbsp curry powder

1 large tomato, chopped

1 sprig fresh thyme, chopped

2 14-oz cans goongo peas

1½ cups water

1 whole Scotch bonnet pepper

10 to 12 spinners (p. 140)

In a large skillet over medium heat, sauté onions, escallion, and garlic and for 2 minutes.

Add curry powder, tomatoes, and thyme and cook for another 2 minutes.

Stir in peas, water, Scotch bonnet pepper, and spinners.

Cover and cook for 15 to 20 minutes.

Remove Scotch bonnet pepper before serving.

Serves 4 to 6.

For a non-vegetarian variation, add 1 lb minced beef after sautéing onions and garlic. Brown beef well before adding remaining ingredients.

GOONGO PEAS & RICE

The Scotch bonnet pepper flavors the rice. Be careful not to break the pepper, as it will make the rice too spicy.

4 cups water
1 19-oz can goongo peas
1 stalk escallion, chopped
1 small onion, chopped
1 sprig of thyme, chopped
2 tsp salt
1 tsp black pepper
1 clove garlic, chopped
2 cups coconut milk (p. 21)
1 whole Scotch bonnet pepper
3 cups uncooked white rice

In a large saucepan, bring water to boil. Add all ingredients except
    Scotch bonnet pepper and rice and boil for 15 minutes.
Add whole pepper and cook another 2 minutes.
Stir in rice. Lower heat, cover, and steam for 25 minutes.
Remove Scotch bonnet pepper before serving.

Serves 4 to 6.

JEWELLED RICE

Using quality rice is important to making a good rice dish. White rice cooks faster than parboiled rice, so you may need to add extra water if using the latter.

3 cups water
1 cup coconut milk (p. 21)
1 tsp turmeric
1 tbsp salt
½ tsp black pepper
2 tbsp margarine
1 cup mixed vegetables
2 cups uncooked white rice

In a large saucepan, bring water to boil.
Add all ingredients except rice.
Boil for 10 minutes. Stir in rice.
Lower heat, cover, and steam for 25 minutes.

Serves 2 to 4.

SEASONED RICE

Seasoned rice is a side dish for many Jamaican main courses. The curry powder is optional; it does give this dish a different taste. Try both versions, with and without the curry.

2 tbsp vegetable oil
1 stalk escallion, chopped
1 tbsp onion, chopped
½ lb prepared salt cod (see note on p. 17)
3 cups water
1 cup coconut milk (p. 21)
1 sprig fresh thyme
1 tsp salt
½ lb Jamaican pumpkin, peeled, seeded, and diced
2 tbsp margarine
1 whole Scotch bonnet pepper
1 tbsp curry powder (optional)
2 cups uncooked white rice

In a medium saucepan over medium heat, sauté onions
    and cod in oil for 3 minutes.
Add remaining ingredients except the rice.
Boil until pumpkin is cooked, about 15 minutes.
Stir in rice, lower heat, cover, and steam for 25 minutes.

Serves 4 to 6.

Jamaican pumpkin has a taste all its own. You can buy it at West Indian markets, or you can substitute butternut or acorn squash.

RICE & PEAS

Rice & Peas (red kidney beans) is a traditional dish in Jamaica and throughout the Caribbean. Coconut milk is a must when cooking this dish. When I was a child, I used to help select the coconut, then drink the water out of it before breaking the coconut and grating the meat. Of course, by the time the whole process was completed, I'd eaten half the coconut! Today, I always try to cook in the traditional way, but with the fast pace of life, at home, I often use canned coconut milk. –L.

4 cups water

1 19-oz can red kidney beans

2 cups coconut milk (p. 21)

2 tsp salt

1 tsp black pepper

2 stalks escallion, chopped

1 small onion, chopped

1 sprig fresh thyme, chopped

2 tbsp margarine

1 whole Scotch bonnet pepper

3 cups uncooked white rice

In a medium saucepan over high heat, bring water to boil.
Add all ingredients except for the Scotch bonnet pepper and rice.
Boil for 15 minutes. Add Scotch bonnet pepper and cook for another
    2 minutes, then stir in rice.
Cover and steam for 25 minutes, stirring occasionally.
Remove Scotch bonnet pepper before serving.

Serves 4 to 6.

To me, Sunday dinner without Rice & Peas served with Salted Pig Tails just wasn't Sunday dinner at all. Be adventurous and try this wonderful variation!

SALTED PIG TAILS.

Buy pigtails at your local West Indies, Italian, or Portuguese market. Soak them in water overnight in the refrigerator to remove excess salt. Cut tails into 1" pieces before adding tails at the same time you add the beans. When trying this version, add salt to taste when cooking with peas.

STUFFED PUMPKIN

1 small pumpkin or buttercup squash

2 tbsp vegetable oil

1 small onion, chopped

1 clove garlic, chopped

1 tbsp curry powder

¼ tsp black pepper

12 oz salad shrimp or dried shrimp

1 tbsp margarine

2 tbsp bread crumbs

Preheat oven to 375° F.

In a stockpot, blanch whole pumpkin or squash.

With a sharp knife, cut a 3" circle around stem area to create a lid.

Lift out lid and set aside. Using a large spoon, remove all seeds.

In a large, greased baking dish, bake pumpkin, lid on, for 30 minutes.

Remove pumpkin from heat.

Cool slightly, and with a large spoon, scrape flesh from pumpkin.

Set aside both pumpkin shell and flesh.

In a saucepan over medium heat, sauté onions and garlic in oil for 3 minutes.

Stir in curry powder, pepper, and shrimp, reserving 5 shrimp for garnish.

Add pumpkin flesh, pepper, margarine, and bread crumbs and cook for
    another 3 minutes.

To serve, place pumpkin on a large serving dish and garnish with the
    reserved shrimp.

Serves 6.

To get a pumpkin to bake more quickly, oil the outside with olive or
vegetable oil.

SAUTÉED BEANS & ZUCCHINI

This simple dish is one of Ed's favorite side dishes. He likes it served with just about any meat dish, but especially with steak.

2 cups water
¼ lb green string bean, stemmed and halved
¼ lb yellow string beans, stemmed and halved
4 tbsp olive oil
1 small onion, sliced
¼ tsp curry powder
1 medium green zucchini, chopped
1 small yellow zucchini, chopped
1 medium green pepper, seeded and sliced
1 small tomato, cut into wedges
¼ tsp salt
¼ tsp black pepper
1 sprig fresh thyme, chopped

In a medium saucepan, bring water to boil.

Add beans and cook for 4 minutes. Drain beans and set aside.

In a medium saucepan over medium heat, sauté beans, onions, and curry powder in oil for 2 minutes.

Add remaining ingredients and sauté for another 3 to 5 minutes.

Remove thyme before serving.

Serves 4 to 6.

STEAMED CABBAGE

1 small, or ½ large cabbage
1 small tomato, cut into wedges
¼ cup water
2 tsp butter
dash of salt and black pepper

Keeping core intact, slice cabbage from to top to bottom into
   6 wedge-shaped pieces.
In a large saucepan over medium heat, arrange cabbage wedges
   in the bottom.
Layer tomatoes on top, then add water, butter, salt, and pepper.
Cover and steam for 7 minutes.

Serves 4.

STEAMED MIXED VEGETABLES

Potatoes or sweet potatoes can be substituted for the cho cho.

2 tbsp margarine
½ small cho cho, peeled and sliced
1 medium carrot, sliced
1 medium onion, sliced
1 sprig thyme
1 large tomato, cut into wedges
1 lb bok choy, chopped
2 cups cabbage, shredded
1 sachet (cube) vegetable bouillon, dissolved in ½ cup water

In a large saucepan over medium heat, sauté cho cho, carrots,
   onion, and thyme in margarine for 2 minutes.
Add remaining ingredients.
Lower heat, cover, and steam for 5 to 8 minutes.

Serves 4.

STEWED RED BEANS

Whether served with pita bread or over steamed rice, this red kidney bean stew is an easy-to-prepare and hearty dish perfect for lunch or dinner on a cold winter's day.

1 19-oz can red kidney beans
1 small onion, chopped
1 medium tomato, chopped
1 clove garlic, chopped
¼ tsp salt
¼ tsp black pepper
1 stalk escallion
1 sprig fresh thyme, chopped
1 tbsp margarine
1 cup water
10 to 12 spinners (p. 140)

In a large saucepan over medium heat, bring all ingredients, except spinners to a boil.

Lower heat, add spinners, cover, and let simmer for 15 minutes until stew is the consistency of baked beans.

Serves 4.

FRIED PLANTAIN

If you have a sweet tooth, sprinkle the fried plantain with sugar or table syrup.

½ cup vegetable oil
2 plantains, peeled and sliced lengthwise or in circles

In a large, heavy saucepan over high heat, fry plantain on both sides until
golden brown.
Remove plantain from pan and place on paper towels to absorb excess oil.

Serves 4.

PRESSED PLANTAIN

Breakfast, lunch, or dinner, pressed plantain makes a tasty side dish.

2 plantains, peeled and cut into 1" wide circles
¼ tsp salt
1 cup hot water
½ cup corn oil
salt to taste

In a large bowl, cover plantains with salted hot water and let stand for
10 minutes.
Remove plantains from water, pat dry, and set aside.
In a medium saucepan over high heat, fry plantains, four pieces at a time,
until light brown.
Remove from pan and place on paper towels to absorb excess oil.
Take a 24" length of wax paper and fold it in half.
Place plantains between wax paper, place a towel over top (so as not to
burn your hands), and press. (You can also use a pop bottle to press
the plantain.)
Return pressed plantains to pan and fry until golden.
Remove and drain once more.
Sprinkle with salt before serving.

Serves 4.

BAMMY

Bammy is made from cassava, which can be purchased frozen in West Indian markets in packages of 2 or 4. As a child, it was a joy for me to grate cassava, then juice them to extract the starch, which was then dried in the sun to make a powder. When hot water was added, this powder was transformed into a white gel and was used to starch clothes, especially school uniforms. –L.

1 pkg bammy (4 to a pkg)
½ cup milk
½ cup vegetable oil
salt to taste

In a bowl, soak bammies in milk, 3 minutes per side.
Remove and set aside.
In large saucepan over medium heat, fry bammy in oil until golden brown.
    (You can also brush each side with margarine and grill.)
Place on paper towels to absorb excess oil.
Sprinkle with salt before serving.
Serve hot with fried fish.

Serves 2.

ROASTED BREADFRUIT

Breadfruit is seasonal. When it is not fully ripe, it is best to boil it. Ripe breadfruit is always roasted, and for this recipe, only ripe breadfruit will do!

1 3-lb ripe breadfruit
1 tbsp vegetable oil

Preheat oven to 350°F.

Oil breadfruit and, with a knife, make a cross at the top and bottom of the fruit.

The cross at the top and bottom of the breadfruit allows steam to escape while baking. Otherwise, well, you could have an exploding breadfruit on your hands.

Bake on a greased baking sheet for 1½ to 2 hours, until fruit yields to the pressure of your thumb.

Cool slightly, peel, and wrap in a damp dishcloth until you are ready to serve.

To serve, slice thinly, cutting away center core.

Serves 6.

Leftover breadfruit can be deep-fried, sprinkled with salt, and served with breakfast.

BOILED BANANAS

Boiled Bananas are usually served hot with stews or curry dishes.

6 fingers of green banana

4 cups water, or enough to cover bananas

½ tsp salt

1 tsp vegetable oil

Use a paring knife, cut of top and bottoms of bananas, and then make a
straight cut along the outer curve of bananas.

In a medium saucepan, bring water to a boil.

Add salt, oil, and bananas.

Cover and cook for 15 to 20 minutes.

Remove bananas, peel, and serve hot with any stew or curry dish.

Serves 4 to 6.

Adding a tsp of vegetable or a tsp vinegar will keep the water from turning
black due to the amount of iron.

GLAZED CARROTS

¼ cup light brown sugar

4 tbsp orange juice

1 tsp orange rind, grated

2 tbsp butter

½ cup water

4 medium carrots, chopped

2 cups lettuce, finely shredded

Preheat oven to 400°F.

In a bowl, combine sugar, orange juice, orange rind, butter, and water.

In a greased casserole dish, layer carrots on bottom.

Pour sugar and orange juice mixture over top.

Cover and bake for 30 to 40 minutes.

Serve on a bed of shredded lettuce.

Serves 4.

Breads&Snacks

CORNMEAL PORRIDGE

Porridge is an all-time Caribbean favorite. It can be made with a variety of foods: harmony corn (dried corn), green bananas, plantains, bulgar wheat, rice, oats, and cornmeal. In fact, cornmeal porridge is one of the first solid foods Jamaican babies eat. If you like your porridge on the rich and sweet side, use a combination of coconut milk, condensed milk, and evaporated milk.

4 cups water
½ tsp salt
1 cup fine, yellow cornmeal
1 tbsp flour
1 cup milk
1 tsp vanilla extract
¼ tsp cinnamon
¼ tsp almond extract (optional)
condensed milk to sweeten

In a medium saucepan, bring salted water to a boil.

In a bowl, combine cornmeal and flour.

Add milk gradually, stirring to make a smooth paste.

Using a whisk, stir cornmeal paste into the boiling, salted water until all of the paste is incorporated. (In other words, there are no lumps.)

Partially cover pot and cook for 15 minutes.

Stir in the vanilla, cinnamon, and almond, cover, and let simmer for about 15 minutes, or until porridge is cooked.

Remove pot from heat and sweeten porridge with condensed milk.

Serve hot with toast or crackers.

Serves 4.

BANANA / PLANTAIN
PORRIDGE

Banana or plantain, or both in combination, can be used in this porridge.

5 cups water

½ tsp salt

3 medium green bananas or 1 large green plantain

1 cup milk (or coconut milk)

1 tbsp flour

1 tbsp vanilla extract

¼ tsp nutmeg

condensed milk or sugar to sweeten

In a medium saucepan, bring salted water to boil.

In a blender or food processor, purée bananas or plantain with milk.

Add flour and pulse for 30 seconds.

Stir puréed bananas into boiling water.

Lower heat and stir vigorously.

Add vanilla extract and nutmeg, and let simmer for 30 minutes until banana
is cooked.

Remove pot from heat and sweeten porridge with condensed milk or sugar.

Serve hot with toast or crackers.

Serves 4.

BULLAS

Bullas are a popular Jamaican snack food. Serve them with ripe bananas, avocados, or cheese. Buttered bullas is also great its own.

3 cups flour
2 tsp baking powder
½ tsp salt
½ tsp nutmeg
¼ tsp ground allspice
1 cup brown sugar
1 cup lukewarm water
3 tbsp margarine, melted
2 tbsp molasses
flour (for dusting)

Preheat oven to 375°F.
In a large bowl, sift together the flour, baking powder, salt,
    nutmeg, and allspice.
Dissolve the sugar in water.
Combine with melted margarine and molasses and add to flour
    mixture to form a firm dough.
Vigorously knead dough to smoothen.
On a lightly floured surface, roll out until it is about ¼" thick.
Using a 4" cookie cutter, cut out circles and lightly dust with flour.
Bake on a greased baking sheet for about 30 minutes.
Serve warm or at room temperature.

Serves 4 to 6.

ROTI

3 cups flour
1 tsp baking powder
½ tsp salt
1½ cups water
1 tbsp margarine, melted

In a large bowl, sift together flour, baking powder, and salt.

Add the water all at once and mix into a soft dough.

Knead dough until smooth.

Cover with a damp cloth and allow to relax for 30 minutes.

Knead dough again, then divide into 8 equal parts.

Shape each part into a ball.

Cover balls with a damp towel and allow to relax for 15 minutes.

Press dough balls flat, then roll into thin circles.

Brush with melted margarine.

Bake on a lightly greased baking sheet or stone for 5 minutes each side.

Serves 4 to 6.

COCONUT BISCUITS

1¼ cups white flour

¼ lb margarine

1 tsp baking powder

⅓ cup sugar

1 tsp vanilla extract

½ cup unsweetened, desiccated coconut

1 egg

2 tbsp water

Preheat oven to 350°F.

In a large bowl, combine flour, margarine, baking powder,
    sugar, and vanilla extract.

Stir until the mixture looks like bread crumbs.

In a small bowl, soften coconut in water.

Add coconut and egg and mix to form a firm dough.

On a lightly floured surface, roll out dough to a ¼" thickness.

Using a cookie cutter, cut into 2" circles or squares.

Place biscuits on a greased baking sheet and bake for 15 minutes.

Makes about 12 biscuits.

 Once biscuits have been cooled, they can be kept in an airtight container.

COCONUT TOTOES

Totoes were one of my childhood favorites. Mom made totoes twice a week, on Sundays and Wednesdays. In a family of ten kids, food disappeared quickly, so she would always hide mine in the bottom of the cabinet. –L.

2 cups flour
3 tbsp baking powder
½ tsp salt
1 tsp nutmeg
¼ lb margarine
1 cup light brown sugar
2 eggs, beaten
2 tbsp vanilla extract
1 dash almond extract
½ cup milk
2 cups grated coconut
¼ cup raisins (optional)

Preheat oven to 375°F.

In a large bowl, combine flour, baking powder, salt, and nutmeg.

Using a hand mixer, cream margarine and sugar until light and fluffy, and then gradually add the flour mixture.

Add the beaten eggs, vanilla, almond, milk, coconut, and raisins.

Pour the batter into a greased 8" square baking pan and bake for 30 minutes.

Let cool, then cut into squares.

Makes 12 squares.

CASSAVA PONE

1 cup cassava, peeled and grated

2 cups sweet potato, peeled
  and grated

¼ cup flour

¼ cornmeal

1¼ cups coconut milk (p. 21)

1¼ cups light brown sugar

½ tsp nutmeg

1 tbsp vanilla extract

½ tsp salt

¼ cup margarine, melted

Preheat oven to 350°F.

In a large bowl, mix cassava, sweet potato, four, and cornmeal. Set aside.

In a separate bowl, combine coconut milk, sugar, nutmeg, vanilla extract,
    salt, and margarine.

Add coconut milk mixture to cassava mixture and blend well.

Pour the batter into a, greased 8" square baking pan and bake for
    1 to 1¼ hours until pone is firm.

Cut into squares and serve at room temperature.

Serves 6 to 8.

CORNBREAD

2 cups cornmeal

¼ cup flour

2 tbsp baking powder

¼ tsp salt

½ cup light brown sugar

1¼ cups milk

⅓ cup margarine, melted

1 egg

2 tbsp corn syrup

Preheat oven to 350°F.

In a medium bowl, combine cornmeal, flour, baking powder, salt, and sugar.
Set aside

In another bowl, combine milk, egg, and margarine.

Add cornmeal mixture and mix well until batter is smooth.

Pour the batter into a 5" x 9" loaf pan and bake until cornbread is golden
    brown, about 30 minutes.

Serve warm or at room temperature.

Serves 6.

EASTER SPICE BUNS

Jamaicans often call loaves of bread "buns." Although spicy, Easter Spice Buns make a great bread for cheese sandwiches.

3 cups flour
¼ tsp baking powder
1 tbsp baking soda
2 cups hot water
1½ cups brown sugar
4 tbsp margarine
1 lb raisins
¼ lb mixed dried fruit
¼ tsp molasses
¼ tsp salt
1 tsp cinnamon
1 tsp nutmeg
½ tsp ground allspice
3 tbsp water
3 tbsp sugar

Preheat oven to 325°F.

In a large bowl, combine flour, baking powder, and baking soda.

In a medium saucepan, bring water to a boil.

Add sugar, stirring until dissolved.

Lower heat, add margarine, raisins, mixed fruit, molasses, salt, and spices.

Let simmer for 10 minutes.

Remove from heat and let cool.

Add cooled liquid to flour mixture. Stir and blend, but do not over mix.

To glaze buns before baking, combine water and sugar and brush mixture onto buns.

Pour batter into a 5" x 9" greased loaf pan.

Bake for 1 to 1½ hours.

RAINBOW SANDWICH

These colorful sandwiches can be made ahead of time, covered, and refrigerated.

> **2 cups cheddar cheese, grated**
> **¼ onion, grated**
> **3 tbsp butter**
> **dash of hot pepper sauce**
> **pinch black pepper**
> **dash of red and green food coloring**
> **3 slices of bread**

In a medium bowl, combine cheese, onion, butter, hot pepper sauce, and black pepper into a paste.

Separate into 3 equal parts.

Add drops of red food coloring to one batch; green to the second, and leave the third part plain.

Spread the red paste on the first slice of bread, green paste on the second, and the third with the plain.

Make a triple-deck sandwich, then trim edges and cut diagonally or crosswise to get 4 pieces.

Serves 2.

SARDINE SPREAD

> **2 tins sardines**
> **1 tsp onions, finely chopped**
> **1 tbsp celery, finely chopped**
> **2 tbsp mayonnaise**
> **½ tsp hot pepper sauce**
> **pepper to taste**

In a bowl, combine all ingredients.

Serve with crackers, or as a spread for sandwiches.

Serves 4.

SOLOMON GUNDY

Solomon Gundy is served on crackers or bread. It also makes a great fish sandwich.

1½ lb boneless pickled herring
1 medium onion, chopped
1 Scotch bonnet pepper, seeded and chopped (see note on p. 15)
½ cup vegetable oil
½ tsp ground allspice
¼ cup white vinegar

In a medium bowl, cover pickled herring with cold water and soak overnight. Discard water and rinse fish with warm water.
In a food processor or blender, purée all ingredients into coarse paste.
Preserve in jars (see note on p. 16).

You can also use Solomon Gundy with tuna. Just spread one slice of bread with tuna, the other with Solomon Gundy. The blend of flavors is awesome!

FESTIVAL

Festival is the cousin of the dumpling!

1 cup flour
½ cup cornmeal
1 tbsp baking powder
¼ tsp salt
3 tbsp sugar
2 tbsp milk
¾ cup water
1 cup vegetable oil

In a medium bowl, combine flour, cornmeal, baking powder, salt, and sugar.

In a separate bowl, combine milk and water.

Make a well in center of the flour mixture, then pour in milk mixture.

Using a spoon, mix well, then knead into a soft dough.

Cut into 12 equal pieces and roll lengthwise.

In a deep-fat fryer or heavy saucepan, heat oil to 360°F.

Deep-fry pieces until golden brown.

Drain on paper towels to remove excess oil. Serve hot.

Serves 6 to 8.

FRIED DUMPLINGS

Dumplings are usually eaten with Jerk Chicken (p. 99), Jerk Pork (p. 78), Ackee and Codfish (p. 48), or just by themselves. Dumplings are a favorite with both vegetarians and meat lovers.

3 cups flour
3 tbsp baking powder
3 tbsp sugar
1 tsp salt
½ cup milk
¾ cup water
2 cups vegetable oil

In a large bowl, combine flour, baking powder, sugar, and salt.
Make a well in the center of the flour mixture, then pour in milk and
    ½ of the water.
Using a spoon, mix well, then knead into a soft but firm dough.
Add remaining water if dough is too dry.
Let dough sit for 15 minutes, then cut into 6 to 8 equal parts.
Roll dough lengthwise until they are 1" round, then tie each piece into
    a knot, or just leave round.
In a deep-fat fryer or heavy saucepan, heat oil to 360°F.
 Deep-fry dumplings until golden.

Makes 12 dumplings.

BOILED DUMPLINGS
& SPINNERS

This simple list of ingredients can be used for either dumplings or spinners, depending on which instructions you use.

2 cups flour
¼ tsp salt
1½ cups water (for dough)
6 cups water (for boiling)

For dumplings:
In a large bowl, combine flour, salt, and enough water to a make a stiff dough.
Knead until the dough is smooth.
In a medium saucepan, bring water to boil.
Using the palm of your hand, form dough into balls, then press flat to about
     ½" thick and 3" round.
Boil in water for 15 minutes.

Makes 12 large dumplings.

For spinners:
Instead of forming dough into balls, pinch off about 1" of dough and, using
     the palm of your hand, shape lengthwise to form a thin dumpling about
     2 to 3" long.
Instead of boiling in water, drop the spinners into soups or stews
     approximately 15 minutes before serving.

Makes about 36 spinners.

To make cornmeal dumplings or spinners, substitute 1½ cups flour and ½ cup cornmeal for the 2 cups of flour.

COCONUT CHIPS

5 cups fresh coconut meat (1 medium coconut)
1 tbsp grated ginger
1¼ lbs white sugar
¼ tsp salt
1 cup water

To prepare the coconut, poke out the eyes with a clean screwdriver or ice pick.
Drain the coconut water inside.
Using a hammer, smash the coconut into half a dozen pieces.
With a paring knife, pry meat away from the shell and trim brown, hairy skin
    from the meat.
Using a mandolin, or a food processor fitted with a slicing blade, cut coconut
    pieces into thin chips.
In a heavy saucepan over medium heat, combine all ingredients and cook for
    20 to 30 minutes or until the mixture becomes very sticky.
Remove from heat.
Spoon mixture onto a greased baking sheet.
Cool and serve.

Serves 8 to 10.

SWEET POTATO FRIES

Choose slender sweet potatoes when making fries; they are easier to work with.

1 lb sweet potatoes, peeled
2 cups water
½ tsp salt
½ cup oil

In a large saucepan, boil sweet potatoes for 4 minutes.
Remove from water and set aside to cool.
When cool, cut sweet potatoes in half, then into thin slices.
In a large skillet, heat oil over high heat.
Add sweet potato slices and fry until crispy and golden brown.
Drain on paper towel to remove excess oil.
Serve hot, sprinkled with salt.

SPICY CORN ON THE COB

A tasty idea to try when corn season hits.

6 ears of corn

2 tbsp lime juice

6 tbsp margarine, melted

½ tsp cayenne pepper

¼ tsp salt

¼ tsp black pepper

dash of paprika

Peel leaves from corn, leaving the last 6 leaves on the cob.
Pull these leaves back to expose corn. Set aside.
Preheat barbecue to 300°F.
In a bowl, combine lime juice, margarine, and spices.
With a pastry brush, brush mixture on corn. Pull leaves over cobs.
Then barbecue or grill until corn is cooked, about 15 to 20 minutes.
Remove charred husks before serving.

Serves 6.

You can remove all the leaves from the cobs and roast, basting with the sauce.

TAMARIND BALLS

1 pkg tamarind flesh

1 lb white sugar

¼ tsp hot pepper sauce (optional)

sugar for rolling

In a large bowl, combine tamarind, sugar, and hot pepper sauce.
Roll into balls, then roll in sugar.

Makes 36 balls.

Desserts

SHORT CRUST PASTRY

This crust is great for coconut, plantain, or pineapple tarts.

1 lb flour
½ tsp salt
½ lb unsalted margarine
¼ cup water

In a large bowl, sift together flour and salt.
Using fingertips or a pastry cutter, blend margarine into flour
    until the mixture is crumbly.
Add water gradually, and mix lightly to form dough.
Wrap dough in plastic and refrigerate until ready to use.
When ready to use, remove from refrigerator and let come to
    room temperature.

PIE CRUST PASTRY

1 lb flour
½ tsp salt
¼ cup vegetable shortening
3 tbsp ice water

In a large bowl, sift together flour and salt.
Use fingertips or a pastry cutter, blend margarine into flour,
    until the mixture is crumbly.
Add water gradually, and mix lightly to form dough.
Roll out dough on a lightly floured surface.
Transfer dough to a 9" pie plate. Trim excess.

To bake unfilled, preheat oven to 375ºF.
Prick the pie shell with a fork all over, then bake until light brown,
    about 12 to 15 minutes.

To bake filled, prick the bottom of the shell before filling to prevent
    pastry from puffing up.
Pour in filling and bake pie according to recipe instructions.

BANANA CUSTARD PIE

FILLING:

2 tbsp cornstarch

1 cup white sugar

3 eggs, beaten

1 egg yolk, beaten

1½ cups cereal cream

2 tsp vanilla extract

2 tbsp Jamaican white rum
  (optional)

1½ very ripe bananas, mashed

1 banana (for topping)

apricot jam (for glazing)

PASTRY:

½ cup icing sugar

2 ozs butter

2 egg yolks, beaten

1 tsp vanilla extract

1 cup flour

For pastry:

In a medium bowl, blend icing sugar and butter until crumbly.

Stir in beaten yolks and vanilla extract. Add flour and blend.

On a lightly floured surface, knead lightly until dough is formed.

Wrap dough in plastic and refrigerate until well chilled.

On a lightly floured surface, roll out dough.

Place in the bottom of a 9" pan with removable bottom.

Chill until ready to use.

For filling:

Preheat oven to 350°F.

In a large bowl, combine cornstarch and sugar.

Add beaten eggs and beaten egg yolk and blend well.

Add cream, rum, and vanilla extract and mix until smooth.

Stir in bananas.

Pour mixture into chilled pie shell and bake at for 20 minutes.

Lower oven temperature to 325°F and bake 10 to 15 minutes
    until custard is set.

Remove from oven and cool.

To serve: slice 1 banana into rounds and place around outer
    edge of pie in a circle.

Broil until golden brown.

Glaze with warm apricot jam and chill before serving.

COCONUT CREAM PIE

You can use my pie crust pastry recipe if you like. But at home, I often just use a ready-made bought shell.

2 cups milk

⅓ cup sugar

3½ tbsp cornstarch

1 tsp vanilla extract

6 egg yolks

1 cup whipping cream

1 tbsp Jamaican white rum (optional)

1¼ cups toasted coconut

9" baked pie shell (p. 144)

Using a double-boiler, heat milk and sugar.

In a bowl, combine cornstarch, vanilla, and egg yolks, and beat lightly.

Slowly add hot milk and sugar mixture and blend well.

Using a sieve, strain liquid into a saucepan and cook until thick.

Remove from heat, cover with wax paper, let cool, and refrigerate.

Whip heavy cream and fold into cooled mixture.

Add rum (if desired), and fold in 1 cup toasted coconut.

Pour mixture into pie shell and cover with remaining coconut.

Chill before serving.

To toast coconut, reheat oven to 350°F. Line baking tray with wax paper. Sprinkle coarse, desiccated, sweetened coconut onto tray. Bake for 5 minutes until light brown in color. Remove from pan; set aside to cool.

SWEET POTATO PIE

2 cups cooked sweet potatoes

2 eggs, beaten

½ cup brown sugar

⅓ cup flour

¼ cup evaporated milk

½ tsp salt

1 tbsp vanilla extract

1 tsp ground nutmeg

3 drops almond extract

1 unbaked 9" pie shell (p, 144), or ready-made shell

Preheat oven to 350°F.

In a large bowl, mash cooked sweet potatoes.

Add remaining ingredients. Mix well.

Pour mixture into unbaked pie shell.

Bake until filling is firm, about 45 minutes.

PUMPKIN PIE

2 cups cooked pumpkin

1 cup cooked sweet (Canadian) yam

1 egg

¼ cup brown sugar

1 tsp cinnamon

¼ tsp ground nutmeg

1 tbsp molasses

1 tbsp vanilla extract

¼ tsp salt

3 tbsp flour

⅓ cup evaporated milk

⅓ cup milk

1 unbaked 9" pie shell (p. 144), or ready-made shell

Preheat oven to 350°F.

In a large bowl, mash cooked pumpkin and yams together.

Add remaining ingredients and mix well.

Pour filling into unbaked pie shell and bake pie for 30 minutes
    or until knife in center comes out clean.

To serve, top with whipped cream or vanilla ice cream.

Serve warm or cold.

MANGO & PINEAPPLE CHEESECAKE

CRUST:

1½ cups graham cracker crumbs

2 tbsp white sugar

⅓ cup melted butter

FRUIT:

⅓ cup water

2 tbsp sugar

¼ tsp lime juice

¼ cup mango, cut into chunks

¼ cup pineapple chunks,
   fresh or canned

FILLING:

½ cup pineapple juice

1 envelope unflavored gelatin powder

1 cup sugar

2 whole eggs

2 eggs, separated

¼ tsp lime zest, grated

1 cup whipping cream

2 8-oz pkgs soft cream cheese

To prepare crust:

In a bowl, combine graham cracker crumbs, sugar, and melted butter.

Press mixture onto the bottom and ½" up sides of a 9" spring form pan.

To prepare fruit:

In a saucepan over low heat, combine water, sugar, and lime juice
   until the sauce and let simmer just begins to thicken.

Add mango and pineapple chunks into the sauce. Let simmer for 2 more minutes.

Remove fruit chunks from the sauce and chill.

To prepare filling:

In a saucepan, combine pineapple juice and gelatin.

Let stand for five minutes to soften.

Stir in sugar, eggs, egg yolks, and grated lime zest.

Cook over low heat, stirring constantly, until the sugar and gelatin dissolve.

Set aside. In a bowl, using a mixer or hand beater, cream cheese until smooth.

Gradually add one half of the gelatin mixture and beat until smooth.

Then stir in remaining mixture along with the fruit chunks.

Cover with plastic wrap, refrigerate about 1 hour until slightly thickened.

Remove filling from fridge. Beat egg whites until soft peaks form.

Using a hand mixer or mix master, beat whipping cream.

Fold whipped cream and egg whites together, then blend cream cheese
   into fruit mixture.

Pour into crust.

Refrigerate for about 4 hours or until set.

MARBLE CHEESECAKE

PASTRY:

1 cup graham cracker crumbs

1 tbsp sugar

¼ cup butter, melted

FILLING:

8-oz pkgs cream cheese, at room temperature

¾ cup sugar

3 eggs

2 tsp vanilla extract

1 oz chocolate, melted

For pastry:

Preheat oven to 350°F.

In a bowl, combine crumbs, sugar, and butter.

Press into bottom of a 9" spring form pan and chill for ten minutes.

Bake for 10 minutes. Cool before using.

For filling:

Preheat oven to 350°F.

In a blender or food processor, lightly beat cream cheese and sugar.

Add eggs one at a time, beating after each egg until smooth.

Add vanilla extract and mix well.

Transfer ³/₄ cup of the batter to a separate bowl.

Blend in melted chocolate.

Pour remaining batter into prepared crust.

Add chocolate batter to center of pan.

Using a knife, swirl chocolate batter into filling.

Bake for 5 minutes.

Lower temperature to 200°F and bake for another 45 minutes.

Chocolate burns quickly, so melt it in the microwave or in a small double-boiler.

BAKED BANANAS

Serve warm or at room temperature with ice cream, chilled evaporated milk, or Coconut Cream (p. 154).

4 ripe bananas, peeled
1 tbsp butter
3 tbsp brown sugar
1 tbsp white rum
3 tbsp milk

Preheat oven to 350ºF.
Cut bananas into halves, lengthways.
Arrange in a buttered, ovenproof dish.
Sprinkle sugar and drizzle rum over bananas.
Pour on milk and bake for 20 minutes.

Serves 4 to 6.

COCONUT PUDDING SURPRISE

1 6-oz pkg coconut pudding mix
1 cup graham cracker crumbs
1 8-oz can mandarin oranges, drained
½ cup pineapple chunks, drained
Toasted coconut, whipping cream, and cherries (garnish)

Prepare coconut pudding mix according to instructions on the package.
Cover bottom of a 9" ceramic pie dish with graham cracker crumbs,
    then layer with mandarins and pineapple chunks.
Pour pudding mix on top.
Cover loosely with a sheet of wax paper to prevent a skin from forming
    and refrigerate overnight.
To serve, cut into squares.
Dust serving plate with toasted coconut.
Top squares with whipping cream and cherries.

SWEET POTATO PUDDING

Sweet potato pudding is known and loved by all Jamaicans. I could not wait to get home at lunch to enjoy some of my mom's pudding. Sweet potato pudding with a glass of milk will keep you full all day. You can serve this pudding hot or at room temperature and topped with whipped cream or ice cream. —L.

2 lbs sweet potatoes, grated

¼ lb yellow yams, grated

½ cup flour

¼ cup cornmeal

½ cup raisins

4 cups coconut milk

1 cup brown sugar

1 tsp nutmeg

½ tsp salt

2 tbsp vanilla extract

2 tbsp white rum (optional)

¼ cup melted butter

Preheat oven to 350°F.

In a large bowl, mix together the sweet potatoes, yams, flour, cornmeal, and raisins. Set aside.

In a medium bowl, combine coconut milk and brown sugar.

Then add nutmeg, salt, vanilla extract, rum, and melted butter.

Pour into potato mixture. Beat until smooth.

Pour batter into a greased 9" baking pan.

Allow to rest for 10 minutes, then bake for 1 to 1¼ hours until pudding is a bit soft but firm.

This recipe can also be used to make blue draws, otherwise known as "tie-a-leaf" or "ducono," which is potato pudding mixture wrapped into banana leaves (available at Asian markets) and then boiled in water. To prepare leaves, cut each leaf along its spine, then cut into a 6" square. Spoon batter in the center of the leaf, then fold leaf like a package, and tie with string. Place in boiling water and cook for 20 to 30 minutes. Serve warm or cold.

CORNMEAL & CURRANT PUDDING

This is another pudding that can be served hot or cold and topped with whipped cream or ice cream.

2 cups cornmeal
2 cups sweet yams, grated
1 cup flour
¼ cup carrots, grated
1½ cups evaporated milk or coconut milk (p. 21)
1½ cups sugar
1 tbsp vanilla extract
2 tbsp butter, melted
1 tsp ground nutmeg
1 tsp salt
½ cup dried currants

Preheat oven to 350°F.

In a medium bowl, combine cornmeal, yams, flour, and carrots.

In a separate bowl, mix the coconut milk with the sugar, vanilla extract, and melted butter. Stir well.

Mix in cornmeal mixture, nutmeg, salt, and currants.

Pour into a 10" round baking pan and bake for 1 to 1¼ hours until pudding is a bit soft but firm.

MANGO DELIGHT

Great served warm or with a scoop of vanilla ice cream.

1 large mango, ripe and firm
½ tsp freshly squeezed lime juice
½ tsp freshly squeezed orange juice
4 tbsp sugar
4 tbsp water
1 tbsp orange liqueur (optional)

Peel the mango and then slice it crossways, cutting it away from the pit.
Set the mango slices aside.
In a saucepan over medium-high heat, combine lime juice, orange juice,
    sugar, and water and cook until sauce thickens, stirring often.
As the sauce thickens, add mangoes and orange liqueur.
Cook for another 3 to 5 minutes.

Serves 2.

EGG CUSTARD

This custard can be served warm or cold with a sprinkling of icing sugar and
cinnamon and a dollop of whipped cream.

4 cups milk
½ cup sugar
4 eggs
¼ tsp salt

¼ tsp vanilla extra
½ tsp white rum
dash of nutmeg

Preheat oven to 350°F.
Warm milk and set aside.
In a medium bowl, combine milk with remaining except nutmeg and beat well.
Pour custard into 4 oz custard cups.
Place cups in a shallow pan of hot water, about 1" deep.
Sprinkle custard with the nutmeg.
Bake for 30 to 40 minutes until custard is firm but soft.

PONCHE DE CRÈME

6 eggs
1 tsp lime zest
3 10-oz cans evaporated milk
1 10-oz can condensed milk
½ cup Jamaican or Trinidadian rum
1 tsp. Angostura bitters
¼ tsp grated nutmeg

In a bowl, beat eggs with lime zest until light and fluffy.
Add evaporated milk, condensed milk, rum, bitters, and nutmeg and mix well.
Refrigerate. Serve over crushed ice.

Serves 4 to 6.

COCONUT CREAM

1 pkg unflavored gelatin
½ cup water
1½ cup coconut milk (p. 21)
½ 10-oz can condensed milk
pinch salt
¼ tsp nutmeg (garnish)

In a medium saucepan over low heat, dissolve gelatin in water.
Stir in coconut milk and remove from heat.
Sweeten with condensed milk and salt.
To serve, pour into dessert dishes, sprinkle with nutmeg, and chill.

Serves 2 to 4.

PINEAPPLE TURNOVERS

You can serve these turnovers hot or at room temperature. For extra sweetness, sprinkle them with white sugar.

1 19-oz can pineapple chunks
2 tsp lemon juice
⅓ cup brown sugar
2 tbsp orange juice
2 tbsp cornstarch
1 Short Crust Pastry (p. 144)
milk for brushing tops of patties

Preheat oven to 350°F.

Discard half the liquid from can of pineapple.

In a food processor or blender, purée the pineapple chunks with the remaining liquid from can until smooth.

In a medium saucepan over low heat, combine puréed pineapple with lime juice, sugar, orange juice, and cornstarch.

Let simmer for 15 to 20 minutes until texture is jelly-like.

On a lightly floured surface, roll out pastry.

With a 4" pastry or cookie cutter, cut into circles.

Spoon pineapple filling onto half of each circle and fold to form half-moon shapes.

Seal edges and crimp with a fork.

Prick tops of patties with fork.

Brush with milk and bake for 15 minutes.

Serves 12.

COCONUT SQUARES

CRUST:

½ cup butter, softened

¼ cup light brown sugar

1 cup flour, sifted

TOPPING:

1 cup fine, desiccated coconut

2 eggs, beaten

½ tsp salt

1 tsp vanilla extract

4 tbsp flour

½ cup brown sugar

1 cup chopped nuts

For crust:

Preheat oven to 375°F.

In a medium bowl, cream butter and sugar until fluffy. Mix in flour.

Pour into a 9" square baking pan and bake for 10 to 12 minutes.

For topping:

Preheat oven to 375°F.

In a medium bowl, combine all ingredients, and mix well.

Spread evenly over crust.

Bake for 20 minutes.

Cool before cutting into squares for serving.

COCONUT MACAROONS

2 egg whites

½ cup white sugar

1½ cup grated coconut

½ tsp vanilla extract

½ tsp Jamaican white rum

Preheat oven to 350°F.

Using a mix master or hand beater, beat egg whites until they form stiff peaks.

Fold sugar carefully into the egg whites.

Add coconut, vanilla, and rum.

Using a tablespoon, drop mixture on a greased baking sheet.

Bake for 15 to 20 minutes until just lightly brown on top.

COCONUT BREAD

4 cups flour

2 tsp baking powder

½ tsp salt

2 cups grated coconut

¾ cup sugar

1 tsp vanilla extract

1 egg, beaten

¼ cup raisins

1 cup milk

sugar for sprinkling

Preheat oven to 350ºF.

In a large bowl, sift together flour, baking powder, and salt.

Mix in coconut, sugar, vanilla, beaten egg, and raisins.

Add milk to mixture a bit at a time, to make a firm but not sticky dough.

Knead dough for a few minutes, then shape into two loaves.

Bake loaves in greased 5" x 9" loaf pans for about 1 hour.

Remove from oven and sprinkle with sugar.

Serve warm or at room temperature.

BANANA FRITTERS

1 cup ripe banana, mashed

1 egg

⅓ cup white sugar

1 tsp vanilla extract

¼ tsp salt

pinch of ground nutmeg

⅓ cup milk

1 cup flour

½ cup vegetable oil

white sugar (garnish)

In a medium bowl, combine banana, egg, sugar, vanilla, salt, nutmeg, and milk.

Add flour and stir to form a smooth batter.

In a medium saucepan over high heat, spoon batter, one tablespoon at a time,
    into hot oil and fry about 3 minutes each side, until golden brown.

Drain on paper towels to absorb excess oil.

Sprinkle with white sugar before serving.

Serves 2.

BANANA BREAD

1 stick butter

1 cup sugar

1 tsp almond extract

1 tsp vanilla extract

½ cup milk

3 eggs

2 cups flour

1 pinch salt

2 tsp. baking powder

1 tsp ground nutmeg

3 ripe bananas, mashed

Preheat oven at 350°F.

In a large bowl, combine butter, sugar, almond, vanilla, and milk and mix
    well until light and fluffy, then add eggs one at a time, mixing well
    after each addition.

In a separate bowl, mix flour, salt, baking powder, and nutmeg.

Combine flour mixture with liquid ingredients.

Add bananas and mix well.

Pour batter into an 8" greased pan.

Bake bread for 45 minutes or until a toothpick inserted into center
    comes out clean.

RUM CAKE

Making Rum Cake is a labor of love for me. The first thing we do on Christmas morning is to thank the Lord for his gift of life, then we eat a slice of Rum Cake accompanied by a glass of Sorrel Drink (p. 167). That's our family tradition. –L.

CAKE:

1 cup port wine

¼ cup white rum

1 lb butter

¾ lb brown sugar

8 large eggs, beaten

2 tbsp vanilla

3 tbsp browning

1 tbsp lime juice

1¼ lb flour

2 tbsp baking powder

1 tbsp ground nutmeg

¼ tsp ground allspice (optional)

¼ tsp cinnamon powder

1 tbsp lime zest

FRUIT:

1¼ lbs raisins

½ lb currants

½ lb pitted prunes

¼ lb mixed fruits

½ cup white rum

3 cups port wine

For fruit:

In a large saucepan over low heat, combine all ingredients.

Steam for 10 minutes to soften fruit. Cool. In a food processor, blend coarsely.

Put into sterilized jars (see note on p. 16). Store in a cool place until ready to use.

For cake:

Preheat oven to 325°F. Combine port and rum and set aside.

In a medium bowl, using a mixer, cream butter and sugar until fluffy.

Add in eggs, one at a time, mixing well after each addition.

Mix in vanilla, browning, and lime juice, and set aside.

In a separate bowl, combine flour, baking powder, nutmeg, allspice, cinnamon, and lime zest. Mix half the flour mixture into the butter mixture, then add all the fruits, followed by remaining flour mixture.

Grease and line bottom of two 9" pans with wax paper.

Pour cake batter into tins and bake for 45 minutes to 1 hour. Cool pans on a cake rack. Remove cakes. Pour port and rum mixture over each cake.

Wrap cakes in plastic wrap, then with foil. Keep stored in a cool place.

Rum cakes keep up to 2 months if you keep adding rum mixture to it.

RAINBOW CAKE

A colorful and delicious cake that the kids just love.

3 cups flour
2 tbsp baking powder
½ tsp salt
8 oz butter
8 oz sugar
4 eggs, beaten
1 tsp vanilla extract
1 cup milk
1 tbsp cocoa powder
red food coloring

Preheat oven to 350°F.

In a large bowl, sift together flour, baking powder, and salt.

In another bowl, cream butter and sugar.

Gradually add beaten eggs to creamed mixture. Mix until fluffy.

Add vanilla extract.

Add flour mixture and milk alternately to creamed mixture.

Divide batter in half.

Pour one half the batter into a greased 10" cake pan.

Halve remaining batter once again.

Add cocoa powder to one half; drops of red food coloring to the other.

To the plain batter in the pan, pour cocoa batter first into the center of the pan.

Then pour red batter, forming a circle around the cocoa batter.

Use a knife to swirl around.

Bake for 45 minutes to 1 hour.

Cool and serve.

GRATER CAKE

2 cups coconut, freshly grated
1¼ cup brown sugar
½ cup water
pinch salt
½ tsp fresh ginger, grated (optional)

In a heavy saucepan over high heat, combine all ingredients.
Boil until coconut is cooked and the liquid has evaporated.
Mixture should be sticky and able to hold together.
Pour mixture into a 9" square baking pan, using a spatula to press into shape.
Cool then cut into squares.

MATRIMONY

We only make this unusual fruity dessert at Christmas time.

3 medium grapefruit, halved
2 small oranges, halved
½ cup condensed milk
¼ tsp grated nutmeg
1 tbsp orange liqueur (optional)
white sugar (garnish)

Cut segments from grapefruit and oranges, leaving skins intact.
Set skins aside.
In a bowl, combine fruit segments, condensed milk, nutmeg, and orange liqueur.
Fill grapefruit skins with mixture, then gently wrap in plastic wrap.
Place in freezer and let freeze for about 45 minutes.
Decorate serving plates by cutting orange skins into fancy designs.
Sprinkle plates lightly with sugar and serve Matrimony on top.

Serves 6.

PUMPKIN COOKIES

2 cups white sugar

½ cup shortening

2 eggs, beaten

2½ cups cooked pumpkin, mashed

1 tsp baking soda

1 tbsp vanilla extract

¼ tsp molasses

4 cups flour, sifted

3 tbsp baking powder

1 tsp salt

1½ cups raisins

½ tsp ginger powder

½ tsp cinnamon

½ tsp ground allspice

Preheat oven to 375°F.

In a food processor or mixing bowl, cream sugar and shortening.

Add beaten eggs, pumpkin, baking soda, vanilla, and molasses.

Blend well.

In a large mixing bowl, combine flour, baking powder, salt, raisins, and
remaining spices.

Mix into creamed mixture and spoon batter onto greased baking sheets.

Bake for 10 to 12 minutes.

Makes 4 dozen cookies.

Drinks

MANGO SHAKE

This is a great shake to make with your kids.

1 cup 2% milk
1 scoop vanilla or mango ice cream
½ cup ripe mango, diced

1 dash vanilla extract
sprinkle of ground nutmeg

In a blender, purée all ingredients. Serve immediately in chilled glasses.

SKY JUICE

This colorful frozen concoction will send you sky-high!

3 cups water
1 large orange, juiced
1 medium lime, juiced
¼ cup strawberry or cherry syrup
Sugar to taste

In a large bowl, combine all ingredients.
Fill medium-sized plastic sandwich bags halfway with mixture. Tie tightly.
Freeze until solid.
To serve: Cut a hole at the tip and suck like a Popsicle.

PEANUT PUNCH

1 cup 2% milk
½ cup smooth peanut butter
1 can condensed milk
2 tbsp cornstarch

5 cups water
1 tsp grated nutmeg
1 tbsp vanilla extract

In a medium saucepan over low heat, combine milk, peanut butter, condensed
    milk and cornstarch.
Let simmer, stirring constantly for 5 minutes.
Remove from heat, add remaining ingredients, and stir well.
Let cool, then refrigerate before serving.

MILO

Milo is a chocolate drink, much like Ovaltine. It's a nice drink on its own or poured on top of vanilla ice cream.

- **1 cup milk**
- **2 tbsp milo**
- **1 tsp condensed milk or white sugar**

Heat milk, then pour into cup. Stir in milo and sweeten with milk or sugar.

BEDTIME SOOTHER

A sure cure for insomnia.

- **1 cup 2% milk**
- **1 pinch fresh nutmeg, grated**
- **1 tsp condensed milk or white sugar**

Heat milk, then pour into cup. Stir in nutmeg and sweeten with milk or sugar.

PINEAPPLE COOLER

A perfect pineapple drink for the patio.

- **1 medium pineapple, peeled and finely diced**
- **¼ cup lime juice**
- **8 cups water**
- **2 cups light brown sugar**
- **mint and/or lime for garnish**

In a punchbowl, combine pineapple and lime juice. Set aside.
In a large saucepan over medium heat, heat water.
Add sugar and stir until dissolved.
Pour sugar water over pineapple, cover, and let sit until cool.
Blend, then strain through a sieve. Chill.

Serve over crushed ice. Garnish with fresh mint or lime.

CARROT JUICE

When it's summer, I like to enjoy refreshing and good-for-you drinks. This is one of my favorites. –L.

2 cups carrots, diced or grated

2 cups water

1 tsp fresh ginger, grated

2 tbsp fresh lime juice

sugar to taste

In a food processor or blender, purée carrots, ginger, and water.
Strain, then add lime juice and sweeten with sugar.
Serve over crushed ice, garnish with mint.

You can also employ a juicer using 1 cup of juice to 2 cups water.

CARROT JUICE WITH MILK

1 cup carrot juice (above)

2 cups water

¼ cup evaporated milk

½ tsp vanilla extract

pinch of grated nutmeg

condensed milk for added sweetness

Combine carrot juice, water, evaporated milk, vanilla and nutmeg.
Add condensed milk for sweetness.
Chill and serve.

SORREL DRINK

Sorrel is a wonderful, leafy herb that gives this drink its distinctive flavor. Sorrel is a member of the Hibiscus family, and a traditional Christmas drink.

10 cups water
¼ cup fresh ginger, grated
2 pkgs dry sorrel
2 cups sugar

In a large saucepan, boil ginger and water for 5 minutes.
Remove from heat, add sorrel and let sit overnight, then strain and
    discard pulp.
Sweeten with sugar, mix well, and refrigerate in a pitcher.
Serve over crushed ice and garnish with lime.

You can also mix with Jamaican rum to make a Blood Jamaican.

SPICED SORREL DRINK

This spicy variation is quite refreshing on a hot summer day.

2 pkgs dried sorrel
¼ cup fresh ginger, grated
2 cups water
6 whole cloves
1 cinnamon stick
2" of dried orange peel
6 whole pimento (allspice) berries
2 cups sugar
1 cup Jamaican white rum
½ cup port

In a large saucepan, boil water, ginger, and orange peel for 5 minutes.
Remove pan from heat.
Add sorrel, cloves, cinnamon stick, clove and pimento berries.
Let sit overnight. Strain, discarding berries.
Sweeten with sugar and add rum or port, if desired.
Refrigerate. Serve cold over crushed ice.

SEVILLE ORANGE DRINK

Seville oranges are quite sour, but this mix makes a refreshing sweet drink.

1 cup Seville orange juice

2 tbsp lime juice

3 tbsp Tang orange drink mix, sweetened with sugar to taste

6 cups water

In a large pitcher, mix all ingredients together. Refrigerate.
Serve over crushed ice.

PAPAYA PUNCH

1 medium ripe papaya, peeled and diced

1 can evaporated milk

3 cups water

¼ cup condensed milk

dash of ground nutmeg

dash of bitters

In a blender or food processor, purée all ingredients until smooth.
Serve over crushed ice.

HOT GINGER TEA

A soothing cure for the winter blahs.

1 tsp fresh ginger, coarsely grated

1½ cup hot water

¼ tsp lime juice

sugar to taste

In a teapot, mix ginger, water, and lime juice. Steep for 5 minutes.
Sweeten with sugar, to taste.

IRISH MOSS

This healthy drink is made from Irish moss seaweed. It can be found in West Indian and Asian markets. It's rich, thick, and is said to increase a man's stamina!

2 30-g pkgs Irish moss
8 cups water
2 tbsp flax seed
½ tsp salt
1 cup water (additional)
1 19-oz can condensed milk
1 tbsp vanilla extract
½ tsp ground nutmeg
1 tbsp molasses

In a large bowl, wash Irish moss in a bowl of water to remove sand and dust.

In a large saucepan over high heat, combine moss, water, flax seed, salt, and boil uncovered for 30 minutes.

Remove from heat and cool.

Add the extra cup of water to pot.

Loosen moss by hand, then strain through a sieve.

Discard moss mixture.

Cool liquid (it will become gel-like).

In a blender or a food processor, purée liquid with milk, vanilla, nutmeg, and molasses to sweeten.

Serve cold.

A lot of Irish moss is found in Newfoundland. It can be harvested during certain months of the year in Jamaica, but if it is collected outside of the season you could be arrested.

GINGER BEER

Ginger beer is a refreshing tonic that keeps in the refrigerator for 6 weeks.

4 cups water

2 cups fresh ginger, coarsely grated

½ cup fresh lime juice

3 cups brown sugar

2 tbsp cream of tartar

lime wedges (garnish)

In a large saucepan or stockpot, bring water to a boil.

Add ginger and continue boiling for 2 minutes.

Remove pot from heat, add sugar, lime juice, cream of tartar,
    and let stand for 3 hours.

Strain and refrigerate.

Serve cold with lime wedge.

Serves 6.

SHANDY

½ glass sorrel drink (p. 167)

½ glass lager or ginger beer (above)

slice of lime for garnish

Pour over ice and garnish with lime. Serve in chilled glasses.

STOUT GYM

This drink will give you all the energy you need for the whole week – also all the calories!

1 small bottle Guinness or Dragon Stout
3 scoops vanilla ice cream
½ tsp grated nutmeg
1 tsp Jamaican white rum (optional)
1 egg
1 cup milk
4 tbsp condensed milk (optional)

In a blender, purée all ingredients.
Serve over crushed ice.

MANGO TREE

1½ oz Southern Comfort
3 oz mango juice
pineapple wedge (garnish)
Maraschino cherry (garnish)

Combine ingredients in a highball glass filled with ice cubes. Mix well.
Garnish with a pineapple wedge and cherry.

SOUR JAMAICAN

Ting, a popular Jamaican grapefruit drink, gives a unique flavor to many beverages. You can buy Ting in larger supermarkets and, of course, in any West Indian market.

1½ oz Amaretto
4 oz Ting

juice of 1 wedge of lime
orange zest (garnish)

Combine ingredients in a highball glass filled with ice cubes. Mix well.
Garnish with orange zest.

SIN TING

1 oz Jamaican rum (Appleton Rum)
3 oz Ting
lime wedge (garnish)

Combine ingredients in a highball glass filled with ice cubes. Mix well.
Garnish with a lime wedge.
Pour over ice and garnish with lime.
Serve in chilled glasses.

COOL & DEADLY

The sweet guava masks the potent charms of the Jamaican rum!

1 oz Jamaican rum (Appleton Rum)
4 oz guava juice
pineapple wedge (garnish)
Maraschino cherry (garnish)

Pour into highball glass over ice cubes. Stir well.
Garnish with a pineapple wedge and cherry.

HAVANA PASSION

Just like they do it in Jamaica.

1 oz Havana rum (or Appleton rum)
2 oz guava juice
2 oz passion fruit juice
pineapple wedge (garnish)
Maraschino cherry (garnish)

Pour into highball glass filled with ice cubes. Stir well.
Garnish with a pineapple wedge and a cherry.

JAMAICAN SHOOTER

1 oz Jamaican Rum Cream (or Irish Cream Liqueur)
¼ oz Tia Maria
1 dash of vodka

In a shot glass, pour each ingredient carefully, in the order given, so each floats on the preceding one.

LEMONGRASS ICED TEA

This fragrant drink cools the body down on a hot day. Ja name for lemongrass is "fever grass"!

4 cups water
1 22-gram pkg lemongrass
½ cup white sugar (or sweeten to taste)
1 can ginger ale
1 lemon or lime wedge (garnish)

In a medium saucepan, bring water to a boil.
Add lemongrass and continue boiling for 5 minutes.
Remove from heat, cover, and let cool.
Strain and discard lemongrass, then sweeten with sugar and refrigerate.
When ready to serve, pour over ice cubes until glass is half full, then fill the remainder with ginger ale.
Garnish with lemon or lime wedge.

Mint can also be used instead of lemongrass, or you can combine the two.

FRUIT PUNCH

A refreshing tropical soother.

1 398-ml can pineapple chunks
1 medium ripe banana, sliced
½ small papaya, sliced
3 cups water
3 cups pineapple juice
½ cup strawberry or cherry syrup
3 tbsp lime juice
3 dashes angostura bittters (optional)
orange or lime slices (garnish)

In a blender, combine the pineapple, banana, papaya, and water and purée
    into a smooth mixture.
Add pineapple juice and syrup and blend for another minute.
Pour into a container, add lime juice and bitters, and refrigerate.
Serve over crushed ice and garnish with orange or lime slices.

 If your punch is too thick, add extra water as well as syrup to sweeten.

RUM PUNCH

1½ oz Jamaican white rum
4 oz Fruit Punch (above)

In highball glasses over ice, combine rum and fruit punch.
Garnish with orange or lime wedges.

MENU IDEAS

Planning a meal or party based on *The Real Jerk*, but not sure about how to put the menu together? Here are some ideas!

JAMAICAN BREAKFASTS

Ackee and Codfish (p. 48), fried dumplings (p. 139), hard boiled eggs, strips of bacon, slices of avocado

Steamed callaloo (p. 108), fried plantains (p. 123), codfish fritters (p. 50), slices of bread, boiled or poached eggs

Cornmeal porridge (p. 128), toast, fresh mango and pineapple

Enjoy the above with a cup of Jamaican coffee sweetened with condensed milk.

DINNER FEASTS

Jerk lamb chops (p. 98), shrimp Creole (p. 67), jerk chicken pasta (p. 101), stir fry vegetables, steamed rice, fried plantains (p. 123), fruit punch (p. 174)

Curry goat (p. 95), golden fried chicken (p. 103), kingfish stew (p. 62), curry vegetables, carrot juice (p. 166)

Stewed oxtail (p. 96), curry chicken (p. 105), roti shells (p. 131), steamed rice, steamed cho cho and carrots, coleslaw (p. 44)

Coconut shrimp (p. 69), escovitched snapper (p. 59), bammy (p. 124), stewed beef (p. 86), seasoned rice (p. 117)

SUMMER BARBECUE

Jerk chicken (p. 99), jerk pork (p. 78), and/or jerk ribs (p. 82), pepper shrimp (p. 70), fried plantains (p. 123), rice and peas (p. 118), potato and pasta salad (p. 46), green salad.

WEEKLY MENU PLANNER

Sunday: rice and peas (p. 118), ja fried chicken (p.103), curry goat (p. 95), tossed salad, carrot juice (p. 166)

Monday: stewed beef (p. 86), steamed cabbage (p. 121), Sunday's leftover rice and peas

Tuesday: curry chicken (p. 105), steamed rice, boiled bananas (p. 126), tossed salad

Wednesday: chicken soup (p. 33) or pepper pot soup (p. 36), coconut totoes (p. 133).

Thursday: steamed callaloo (p. 108), curry lentils (p. 110), steamed rice, tomato slices

Friday: kingfish stew (p. 62), boiled bananas (p. 126), fried dumplings (p. 139), tossed salad

Saturday: red pea soup (p. 34), sweet potato pudding (p. 151)

GLOSSARY

Acorn squash: a small to medium-sized, acorn-shaped winter squash with an orange-, yellow-, or white-streaked, fluted shell. It has a sweet and nutty flavor and can be used as a substitute for pumpkin, buttercup, or butternut squash. Select acorn squash with as much green on the rind as possible.

Ackee: the national fruit of Jamaica. In North America, it can only be purchased canned because the fresh version can be poisonous if not picked at the right time or properly prepared.

Allspice (also known as Jamaican pepper): a member of the pimento family introduced into the West Indies by the Spanish in the 17th century. The small, brown berry has a flavor that resembles a mixture of cinnamon, clove, nutmeg, ginger, and pepper. It is used ground (and sometimes whole) in both cooking and baking. It is one spice that gives the liqueur, Benedictine, its unique flavor and it's also used in many men's colognes.

Avocado (also known as Alligator pear): a tropical fruit with a single large pit, smooth to rough-textured skin and a green to purplish color. The flesh has a buttery texture and is high in unsaturated fat. It is the main ingredient in Mexican guacamole. Ripe avocados should be soft and yield to gentle pressure.

Baby back ribs: a cut of pork prime loin.

Back ribs: a fabricated cut of the pork primal loin; consists of the ribs cut from the anterior end; also known as country-style spareribs.

Bammy: originating with the Arawaks Indians, this pancake-like bread is usually served with fried fish.

Barbecue: to roast meat slowly over coals or gas-powered grill.

Blanch: to plunge vegetables into boiling water for two to three minutes then into a bowl of ice water to stop the cooking. Blanching preserves the color, texture, and nutritional value of raw vegetables.

Bok choy: a member of the cabbage family, bok choy has long wide, white crunchy stalks with tender, dark green leaves. It can be found in all major supermarkets.

Bone-in: a cut of meat containing the bone.

Boned, boneless: a cut of meat from which the bone has been removed.

Breadfruit: native to West Africa and the West Indies, breadfruit is a starchy fruit commonly used as a vegetable.

Butterfly: to cut food almost in half so that when flattened the two halves resemble butterfly wings.

Buttercup squash: a winter squash that is dark green and evenly striped with sweet, orange flesh. Can be used as a substitute for pumpkin.

Butternut squash: a large, elongated, pear-shaped squash with a smooth butterscotch-colored shell, orange flesh, and a sweet and nutty flavor. It can be a substitute for pumpkin, acorn squash, buttercup squash, or green papaya.

Callaloo: is a dark green, leafy vegetable rich in iron. Comes canned as well as fresh.

Cassava: a starchy, tuberous root common to the West Indies.

Celery root (or celeriac): a turnip-like root vegetable that can be eaten cooked or raw in salads or in fish dishes. Its origin is unknown, but celery root has been around since the 16th century. You can substitute potatoes or eddoes for celery root.

Cho cho: an edible root. Sometimes also called chayote.

Cilantro (also known as Chinese parsley or fresh coriander): an herb with a sharp, fresh flavor used in West Indian, Asian, and Indian cuisine.

Cod: a large family of saltwater fish with a delicate flavor. The lean, white flesh has a firm texture. Cod is available fresh, salted, or smoked.

Coco (also known as taro root): a small, yam-like root used in Jamaican and Asian cooking. It is also known as dasheen and can be found in most supermarkets as well as West Indian and Asian markets.

Condensed milk: evaporated and sweetened milk that comes only in cans.

Cornmeal: dried, ground corn kernels — white, yellow or blue in color – that have a slightly sweet, starchy flavor. Cornmeal is available in three grinds: fine, medium. and coarse, and is used in baking, or as a coating for fried foods.

Crayfish: a crustacean that resembles a small lobster.

Cube: to cut food into small cube shapes, larger than diced, usually about $1/2$ inch.

Cumin: a spice frequently used in Latin American, Oriental, East Indian, and West Indian cooking. Cumin can be purchased in both seed and ground form.

Curry powder: a blend of spices associated with Indian cuisine, the flavor and color of curry powder varies depending on the exact blend. Typical ingredients include black pepper, cinnamon, cloves, coriander, cumin, ginger, mace, and turmeric. Sometimes cardamom, tamarind, fennel seeds, fenugreek and chili powder are added.

Dash: a seasoning measure indicating a scant $1/8$ teaspoon or less.

Deep-fry: to cook in hot fat (about 360°F) that is deep enough for food to float, usually a minimum of 3 inches.

Devein: to remove the black vein running down the curved top of the shelled shrimp.

Dice: to cut food into cubes or pieces about $1/4$ to $3/4$" in size.

Dredge: to coat lightly with a dry ingredient, like flour, sugar, breadcrumbs, or cornmeal.

Dried shrimp: a dried fish product that can be found in West Indian and Asian markets. Can be reconstituted with a small amount of water before adding to dishes, or added dried to soups and stews.

Drizzle: to sprinkle drops of liquid lightly or pour a very fine stream of liquid over food.

Dust: to lightly sprinkle with a dry ingredient, usually flour.

Eddo: a taro, root-like vegetable with origins definitely in the Caribbean. Although you can find eddoes in West Indian markets, taro root (or coco) can now be found in many large, urban supermarkets.

Egg wash: egg yolks or egg whites, mixed with a small amount of water or liquid, used to brush over pastry to add color and shine.

Escallion: a name given to several members of the onion family including a distinct variety called scallion, immature onions (commonly called green onions or spring onions), young leeks, and sometimes the tops of young shallots. In each case, the vegetable has a white base that has not fully developed into a bulb, and green leaves that are long and straight. Both parts are edible. True escallions have a milder flavor, making chives a better substitute than green onions. Scallions are available all year, but are at their peak during spring and summer.

Escovitch (also known in some cultures as sevich): a method of marinating fish or seafood in vinaigrette. It is used a lot in Jamaican cooking and probably originated with the Portuguese, who use this method in many fish dishes.

Evaporated milk: unsweetened canned milk from which 60% of the water has been removed. Whole evaporated milk contains at least 7.9 % butterfat, while the skim version contains less than $1/2$%.

Flake: to use a fork or other utensil to break off pieces or layers of food.

Ginger root: the gnarled, bumpy rhizome of a tropical plant native to China. Available fresh, powdered, preserved, or candied.

Goongo peas (also known as pigeon peas or gongo peas): Green and brown peas. Black-eyes peas or chickpeas make good substitutes.

Grouper: a member of the sea bass family, characterized by its large head and wide mouth.

Guava: a Caribbean fruit eaten raw or used in making jam or beverages.

Grill: to cook food directly over heat.

Jalapeño: a small, hot, green pepper that can be substituted for the much hotter Scotch bonnet pepper.

Jamaican pumpkin: also called West Indian pumpkin or Cuban squash, it is a large, green squash that can be found in West Indian markets and many large supermarkets. Substitutes include pumpkin, acorn squash, or butternut squash.

Jamaican rum: made from sugar cane, Jamaican rum has a distinct taste, and it's known for its high alcohol content. It is used in drinks, in baked goods, and for medicinal purposes.

Jamaican (Yellow) yam: a yellow yam that can be used in a variety of dishes (not to be confused with Sweet Potatoes).

Lentils: pea-like beans that come canned or dried, brown, yellow, or green in color. Rich in Vitamin A and B, they are used in many soups and stews in many different cuisines.

Mandolin: a flat-framed kitchen utensil with adjustable blades for slicing vegetables.

Mango: a tropical fruit originating in India. The fruit is yellow when unripe and red when ripe. It is used in many dishes, chutneys, jams, and beverages.

Milo: a chocolate drink similar to Ovaltine.

Mussels: a mollusk with a black or purplish shell.

Okra: Seedpods of a mallow family plant used as vegetables or to thicken soups and stews. Sometimes called gumbo.

Pikappeppa: a sauce found in West Indian markets and in large supermarkets. HP Sauce makes a good substitute.

Pimiento: an allspice considered to be the highest quality grown in Jamaica.

Plantain: a banana-like vegetable picked and used green.

Prawns: crustaceans similar to shrimp. In many parts of the world, the term is applied to any large shrimp.

Purée: to process a food into a smooth paste, usually with a blender or food processor.

Roti: a flat Indian bread in which Jamaicans wrap curry dishes.

Sauté: to brown or cook a food quickly in a pan over direct heat, usually using a small amount of hot oil or butter.

Scotch bonnet peppers: one of the hotest peppers in the family of chili peppers. (In North America, they are often called Habanera peppers). Care should be taken when handling these peppers. Always use rubber gloves, wash hands thoroughly after handling, and be careful not to inhale the pepper's fumes when blending or simmering in a soup.

Sorrel: an herb with arrow-shaped leaves that has been used in salads and drinks since the 16th century. A popular drink at Christmas in Jamaica.

Simmer: to cook liquid at a temperature just below the boiling point, low enough that tiny bubbles just begin to break beneath the surface around the edge of the pan.

Steam: to cook indirectly by setting food on top of boiling water in a covered pot.

Strain: to separate liquid from solid food by pouring through a strainer or fine sieve.

Sweet potato: originating in Central America, sweet potato has a white flesh. This potato should not be confused with yams, which have yellow or orange fleshes.

Tamarind: the brown pulp of a West African pea plant. Found in West Indian and Asian supermarkets.

Thyme: an herb with small purple flowers and tiny, gray-green leaves; the leaves have a strong, slightly lemony flavor and aroma. It can be used fresh or dried.

Index

Ackee & Codfish 48
Ackee & Codfish Patties 49
Auntie P's Mincemeat Pasta 90
Avocado
    Avocado Dip 26
    Avocado Dressing 30
    Crab & Avocado Salad 43

Baked Bananas 150
Bammy 124
Bananas
    Baked Bananas 150
    Banana Bread 158
    Banana Custard Pie 145
    Banana Fritters 158
Banana/Plantain Porridge 129
Boiled Bananas 126
Barbecued Jerk Ribs 82
Basic White Sauce 23
Beans
    Sautéed Beans & Zucchini 120
    Spicy Mixed Bean Salad 45
Bedtime Soother 165
Beef
    Auntie P's Mincemeat Pasta 90
    Corned Beef Delight 92
    Corned Beef Mash 91
    Corned Beef Omelet 93
    Corned Beef-Stuffed Pasta 92
    Curry Beef 87
    Jamaican Pot Roast 89
    Jerk Meatballs 98
    Steak Jamaican Style 88
    Stewed Beef 86
    Stewed Cow's Foot 97
    Stewed Kidneys 94
    Stewed Oxtail 86
Boiled Bananas 126
Boiled Dumplings & Spinners 140
Breadfruit, Roasted 125
Broccoli & Codfish 54
Brussel Sprouts & Codfish 52
Bullas 130

Cabbage, Steamed 121
Cakes
    Grater Cake 161

Rainbow Cake 160
    Rum Cake 159
Callaloo
    Callaloo Fritters 109
    Callaloo Rice 109
    Cream of Callaloo Soup 37
    Jerk Snapper Stuffed with Callaloo 57
    Steamed Callaloo 108
Carrots
    Carrot Juice 166
    Carrot Juice with Milk 166
    Cool & Creamy Carrot Salad 45
    Glazed Carrots 126
Cassava Pone 134
Celery Root & Codfish, Grilled 55
Cheesecakes
    Mango & Pineapple Cheesecake 148
    Marble Cheesecake 149
Chicken
    Chicken Stock 32
    Chicken Soup at The Jerk 33
    Curry Chicken 105
    Cutting and deboning 15
    Golden Fried Chicken 103
    Ja Fried Chicken 103
    Jerk Chicken 99
    Jerk Chicken Breasts 100
    Jerk Chicken Pasta in Rundown Sauce 101
    Jerk Chicken Wrap 101
    Jerk Cornish Hens 100
    Jerk Wings 102
    Shrimp & Chicken Pasta 68
    Stewed Chicken 104
Coco & Codfish, Mashed 56
Coconut
    Buying and preparing 17
    Coconut Biscuits 132
    Coconut Bread 157
    Coconut Chips 141
    Coconut Cream 154
    Coconut Cream Pie 146
    Coconut Macaroons 157
    Coconut Milk 21
    Coconut Pudding Surprise 150
    Coconut Shrimp 69
    Coconut Squares 156
    Coconut Totoes 133

Index

Codfish
    Ackee & Codfish 48
    Ackee & Codfish Patties 49
    Broccoli & Codfish 54
    Coo Coo 53
    Brussel Sprouts & Codfish 52
    Codfish Fritters 50
    Escovitched Salt Cod 51
    Grilled Celery Root & Codfish 55
    Ham & Codfish 52
    Mashed Coco & Codfish 56
    Preparing salt cod 17
    Steamed Vegetables & Cod 54
Coleslaw 44
Coo Coo 53
Cook-Up Pork Chops 81
Cool & Creamy Carrot Salad 45
Cool & Creamy Salad Dressing 29
Cool & Deadly 172
Cool Green Salad Dressing 29
Corn on the Cob, Spicy 142
Cornbread 134
Corned Beef Delight 92
Corned Beef Mash 91
Corned Beef Omelet 93
Corned Beef-Stuffed Pasta 92
Cornmeal & Currant Pudding 152
Cornmeal Porridge 128
Cornish Hens, Jerk 100
Cow's Foot, Stewed 97
Crab & Avocado Salad 43
Crab Dip 27
Crazy Ribs 84
Cream of Callaloo Soup 37
Creamy Coleslaw 44
Crunchy Shrimp Salad 41
Cucumber Dip 27
Cucumber Salad 42
Curry Beef 87
Curry Chicken 105
Curry Fish 64
Curry Goat 95
Curry Lentils 110
Curry Potatoes 111
Curry Shrimp 66

Deep frying 17
Dipping sauce 25
Dips
    Avocado dip 26
    Crab dip 27
    Cucumber dip 27
    Quick vegetable dip 26
Dumplings
    Boiled Dumplings & Spinners 140
    Fried Dumplings 139

Easter Spice Buns 135
Egg Custard 153
Escovitched Salt Cod 51
Escovitched Snapper 59

Festival 138
Fish
    Ackee & Codfish 48
    Buying 16
    Curry Fish 64
    Escovitched Snapper 59
    Fried Flying Fish 61
    Jerk Salmon Steaks 59
    Jerk Snapper Stuffed with Callaloo 57
    Jerk Swordfish 60
    Kingfish Stew 62
    Salmon Steaks in Tamarind Sauce 60
    Spicy Fish Salad 42
    Steamed Snapper 58
    Stewed Fish at the Jerk 63
Fish Tea 38
Fried Dumplings 139
Fried Flying Fish 61
Fried Plantain 123
Fruit Punch 174

Ginger Beer 170
Ginger Tea, Hot 168
Glazed Carrots 126
Goat
    Curry Goat 95
    Mannish Water 40
Golden Fried Chicken 104
Goongo Pea Stew 114
Goongo Peas & Rice 115
Grater Cake 161

Index

Grilled Celery Root & Codfish 55
Grouper
    Curry Fish 64
    Stewed Fish at the Jerk 63

Ham
    Ham & Codfish 52
    Holiday Ham 85
Havana Passion 172
Holiday Ham 85
Honey-Glazed Baby Back Ribs 83
Hot Ginger Tea 168

Iced Tea, Lemongrass 173
Irish Moss 169
Island Pizza 102

Ja Fried Chicken 103
Jamaican Pot Roast 89
Jamaican Shooter 173
Janga Pasta 70
Jars
    sterilizing 16
Jerk Chicken 99
Jerk Chicken Breasts 100
Jerk Chicken Pasta in Rundown Sauce 101
Jerk Chicken Wrap 101
Jerk Cornish Hens 100
Jerk Lamb Chops 98
Jerk Meatballs 98
Jerk Pork 78
Jerk Pork Chops 80
Jerk Prawns 71
Jerk Rib Sauce 24
Jerk Ribs, Barbecued 82
Jerk Salmon Steaks 59
Jerk sauce 20
Jerk Snapper Stuffed with Callaloo 57
Jerk Swordfish 60
Jerk Turkey 106
Jerk Wings 102
Jerked & Butterflied Jumbo Shrimp 71
Jewelled Rice 116

Kidneys, Stewed 94

Kingfish
    Kingfish Stew 62
    Stewed Fish at the Jerk 63

Lamb Chops, Jerk 98
Lemon & Lime Sauce 25
Lemongrass Iced Tea 173
Lentil Rice 111
Lentils, Curry 110
Lobster & Shrimp Bisque 39

Mangoes
    Buying and pitting 17
    Mango & Papaya Salsa 28
    Mango & Pineapple Cheesecake 148
    Mango Delight 153
    Mango Shake 164
    Mango Tango Salsa 28
    Mango Tree 171
Mannish Water 40
Marble Cheesecake 149
Mashed Coco & Codfish 56
Mashed Pumpkin & Potato 112
Matrimony 161
Meatballs, Jerk 98
Milo 165
Mussels
    Mussels in Coconut Sauce 74
    Mussels in Spicy Sauce 75
    Preparing 17

Oxtail, Stewed 96

Papaya Punch 168
Papaya Salad 46
Pasta
    Auntie P's Mincemeat Pasta
    Corned Beef-Stuffed Pasta 92
    Janga Pasta 70
    Jerk Chicken Pasta in Rundown Sauce 101
    Potato & Pasta Salad 46
    Shrimp & Chicken Pasta 68
    Shrimp Creole Pasta 68
Pastry
    Short Crust Pastry 144
    Pie Crust Pastry 144
Peanut Punch 164

Index

Pepper Pot Soup 36
Pepper Shrimp 70
Peppers
    handling 15
Pie Crust Pastry 144
Pies
    Banana Custard Pie 145
    Coconut Cream Pie 146
    Pumpkin Pie 147
    Sweet Potato Pie 147
Pineapple Cheesecake, Mango & 148
Pineapple Cooler 165
Pineapple Turnovers 155
Pizza, Island 102
Plantain
    Banana/Plantain Porridge 129
    Fried Plantain 123
    Pressed Plantain 123
Ponche de Crème 154
Pork
    Barbecued Jerk Ribs 82
    Cook-Up Pork Chops 81
    Crazy Ribs 84
    Holiday Ham 85
    Honey-Glazed Baby Back Ribs 83
    Jerk Pork 78
    Jerk Pork Chops 80
    Pork Loin in Ginger Sauce 79
Porridge
    Banana/Plantain Porridge 129
    Cornmeal Porridge 128
Potatoes
    Curry Potatoes 111
    Mashed Pumpkin & Potato 112
    Potato & Pasta Salad 46
Pressed Plantain 123
Puddings
    Coconut Pudding Surprise 150
    Cornmeal & Currant Pudding 152
    Sweet Potato Pudding 151
Pumpkin
    Mashed Pumpkin & Potato 112
    Pumpkin Cookies 162
    Pumpkin Pie 147
    Stuffed Pumpkin 119

Quick Vegetable Dip 26

Rainbow Cake 160
Rainbow Sandwich 136
Real Jerk Sauce 20
Red beans/peas
    Red Pea Soup 34
    Rice & Peas 118
    Stewed Red Beans 122
    Vegetable & Red Pea Soup 35
Red snapper
    Escovitched Snapper 59
    Jerk Snapper Stuffed with Callaloo 57
    Steamed Snapper 58
Ribs
    see pork
Rice
    Goongo Peas & Rice
    Jewelled Rice 116
    Lentil Rice 118
    Rice & Peas 118
    Seasoned Rice
    Shrimp Fried Rice 73
Roasted Breadfruit 125
Roti 131
Rum Cake 159
Rum Punch 174
Rundown Sauce 22

Salad dressings
    Avocado Dressing 30
    Cool & Creamy Salad Dressing 29
    Cool Green Salad Dressing 29
    Tamarind Dressing 30
Salads
    Cool & Creamy Carrot Salad 45
    Crab & Avocado Salad 43
    Creamy Coleslaw 44
    Crunchy Shrimp Salad 41
    Cucumber Salad 42
    Papaya Salad 46
    Potato & Pasta Salad 46
    Spicy Fish Salad 42
    Spicy Mixed Bean Salad
    Tangy Coleslaw 44
Salmon
    Jerk Salmon Steaks 59
    Salmon Steaks in Tamarind Sauce 60

Index

Salsas
    Mango & Papaya Salsa 28
    Mango Tango Salsa 28
Salt cod
    See codfish
Sardine Spread 136
Sauces
    Jerk Rib Sauce 24
    Lemon & Lime Sauce 25
    Real Jerk Sauce 20
    Rundown Sauce 22
    Seafood Sauce 22
    White Sauce 23
    Zippy Dipping Sauce 25
Sautéed Beans & Zucchini 120
Scallops with Garlic & Tomatoes 76
Seasoned Rice 117
Seafood Sauce 22
Seville Orange Drink 168
Shandy 170
Short Crust Pastry 144
Shrimp
    Butterflying 17
    Buying and preparing 16
    Coconut Shrimp 69
    Crunchy Shrimp Salad 41
    Curry Shrimp 66
    Janga Pasta 70
    Jerk Prawns 71
    Jerked & Butterflied Jumbo Shrimp 71
    Lobster & Shrimp Bisque 39
    Peeling and deveining 17
    Pepper Shrimp 70
    Shrimp & Chicken Pasta 68
    Shrimp Creole 67
    Shrimp Creole Pasta 68
    Shrimp Fried Rice 73
    Shrimp, Lentil & Chickpea Curry 72
Sin Ting 172
Sky Juice 164
Solomon Gundy 137
Sorrel Drink 167
Sorrel Drink, Spiced 167
Soups
    Chicken Soup at the Jerk 33
    Cream of Callaloo Soup 37
    Fish Tea 38

Lobster & Shrimp Bisque 39
Pepper Pot Soup 36
Read Pea Soup 34
Vegetable & Red Pea Soup 35
Sour Jamaican 171
Spiced Sorrel Drink 167
Spicy Corn on the Cob 142
Spicy Fish Salad 42
Spicy Mixed Bean Salad 45
Spinners, Boiled Dumplings & 140
Steak Jamaican Style 88
Steamed Cabbage 121
Steamed Callaloo 108
Steamed Mixed Vegetables 121
Steamed Snapper 58
Steamed Vegetables & Cod 54
Stewed Beef 86
Stewed Chicken 104
Stewed Cow's Foot 97
Stewed Fish at the Jerk 63
Stewed Kidneys 94
Stewed Oxtail 96
Stewed Red Beans 122
Stout Gym 171
Stuffed Pumpkin 119
Sweet Potato Balls 113
Sweet Potato Fries 141
Sweet Potato Pie 147
Sweet Potato Pudding 151
Swordfish, Jerk 60

Tamarind Balls 142
Tamarind Dressing 30
Tangy Coleslaw 44
Turkey, Jerk 106
Turn Cornmeal 53

Vegetable & Red Pea Soup 35
Vegetable dip 26
Vegetables, Steamed Mixed 121

White sauce 23

Zippy Dipping Sauce 25
Zucchini, Sautéed Beans & 120

THE REAL JERK

is pleased announce that it is now
selling its own products for you to enjoy at home.

The Real Jerk Sauce and
The Real Jerk Barbecue Sauce
are the first to be available; buy them via
The Real Jerk website (*www.therealjerk.com*),
at the restaurant, or soon at major
supermarkets (stay tuned!).

Visit The Real Jerk the next time
you are in Toronto (and if you live in Toronto,
what are you waiting for?):

709 Queen Street East (at Broadview)
Toronto, Ontario, Canada
phone: 416-463-6055
fax: 416-463-1823